DESIGN TOOLS FOR THE

JUDI HARRIS

Merrill
Prentice Hall

INTERNET-SUPPORTED CLASSROOM

Upper Saddle River, New Jersey
Columbus, Ohio

This special edition published by Merrill Education/Prentice Hall, Inc. by arrangement with the Association for Supervision and Curriculum Development.

Vice President and Publisher: Jeffery W. Johnston
Executive Editor: Kevin M. Davis
Editorial Assistant: Amy Hamer
Director of Marketing: Kevin Flanagan
Marketing Manager: Amy June
Marketing Coordinator: Barbara Koontz

This book was printed and bound by Victor Graphics, Inc. The cover was printed by Victor Graphics, Inc.

10 9 8 7 6 5 4 3 2 1
ISBN: 0-13-093061-X

Design Tools for the Internet-Supported Classroom

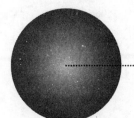

Introduction:

Telecomputing in U.S.

Public Schools

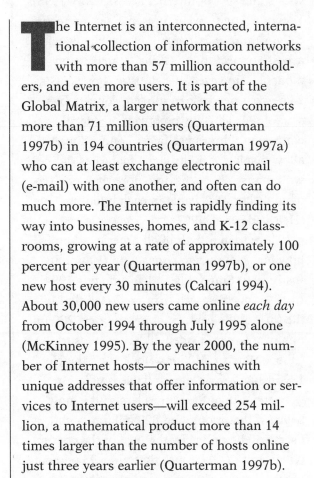

The Internet is an interconnected, international collection of information networks with more than 57 million accountholders, and even more users. It is part of the Global Matrix, a larger network that connects more than 71 million users (Quarterman 1997b) in 194 countries (Quarterman 1997a) who can at least exchange electronic mail (e-mail) with one another, and often can do much more. The Internet is rapidly finding its way into businesses, homes, and K-12 classrooms, growing at a rate of approximately 100 percent per year (Quarterman 1997b), or one new host every 30 minutes (Calcari 1994). About 30,000 new users came online *each day* from October 1994 through July 1995 alone (McKinney 1995). By the year 2000, the number of Internet hosts—or machines with unique addresses that offer information or services to Internet users—will exceed 254 million, a mathematical product more than 14 times larger than the number of hosts online just three years earlier (Quarterman 1997b).

In late 1996, 65 percent of a nationally representative sample of K-12 U.S. educators reported having access to Internetworked telecomputing facilities somewhere in the school building, with 14 percent of that sample having connections in their own classrooms. Secondary schools and larger schools (those with enrollments of 1,000 or more students) were more likely to have Internet access than elementary schools and smaller schools (those with enrollments of 300 students or less) (Heaviside, Riggins, and Farris 1997). More than 40 states now provide public educators with some sort of Internet access (Doty 1995). Yet connectivity, when present, is often technically primitive: 74 percent of all schools with access connect to the Global Matrix using modems. However, this statistic represents a 23 percent decrease in modem connections since 1994. Thirty-two percent of Internet-connected schools use faster connections that allow display of multimedia materials online, with many schools having more than one type of connection available in each building (Heaviside et al. 1997).

More than a sixth of all American homes now house a modem connection (National Institute of Standards and Technology 1994). In 1995, one research firm predicted that by the turn of the century, approximately 200 million people worldwide will have access to the Global Matrix ("Millions Hooked on the Net," 1995). Just a year later, reliable predictions were more than four times larger; it is now believed that more than 800 million e-mail users will be online by the turn of the century (Quarterman 1997b). At that time, 95 percent of all schools will have Internet access (Heaviside et al. 1997), and by 2002, more than 20 million children and teens will be able to use the Internet from their homes (Jupiter Communications, Inc. 1997). The press to provide global connectivity via the Internet to all K-12 classrooms is on, fueled by local, district, state, regional, and national support for the notion of networked interpersonal and information infrastructures.

In late 1996, 97 percent of U.S. public schools with Internet access offered e-mail services to teachers and/or students, and 89 percent made World Wide Web facilities available. Inside the schools with access to the Web, online facilities were most often available for teachers (94 percent of all globally networked schools) and administrative staff (86 percent). Students can use the Web in only 74 percent of all schools reporting Matrix access (Heaviside et al. 1997), but that represents a 20 percent increase in student access from 1995 to 1996. There appears to be a common assumption that giving students (and teachers) access to the vast number and variety of resources available via the Global Matrix is important. As Gallo (1994, p. 18) observes,

> Although the educational benefits of computer networks are still relatively unknown, the prevailing wisdom in some educational technology circles throughout the country is that the K-12 community needs to be connected to a global network and that once connectivity is achieved, K-12 educators will use the resources not currently available within their classroom walls to enhance their institutional programs and achieve specific educational goals. The underlying premise is that if a network is built

that will support educational activities, then every school will want to establish a connection to this network, and teachers in these schools will use the activities to meet the current challenges of education: "If you build it, they will come."

Twenty percent of public school teachers in late 1996 reported using telecommunications for teaching, 16 percent said telecommunications assisted their professional development, and 15 percent stated that telecommunications was part of their curriculum-creation work. Telecommunications training was required in only 13 percent of U.S. public schools in late 1996, but 31 percent of the schools provided incentives for teachers to participate in telecomputing programs at that time. In more than half of the nation's schools, though,

teachers initiated and sustained their telecommunications-related learning and activity without official mandate or encouragement (Heaviside et al. 1997). At this point, it seems that sparking teachers' motivations for *voluntary* use of telecomputing tools is key. Most of the suggestions in this book will be rooted in that assumption.

Although administrators, parents, and teachers all want access to online information and Internet services in K-12 schools, nobody is sure just how this access will serve teaching and learning needs and preferences. We must begin to think seriously about and plan carefully for how to use Internet resources in productive, instructive ways. This is precisely what this book will help you to help teachers to do.

Teachers as
Instructional Designers

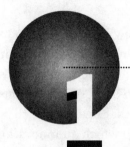

Chances are you've picked up this book because you're preparing to help one or more groups of classroom teachers to design curriculum-based, powerful, and forward-thinking ways for their students to use Internet resources. This is *not* the same as teaching these teachers to use Internet tools, such as electronic mail or a World Wide Web browser. To illustrate the nature of the difference, consider how simple it is to learn to operate a pair of electric hedge clippers. Yet using them to create a decorative garden display requires not only skill with the tool but, more important, an artistic, holistic, and practical grasp of horticultural design.

Teachers who successfully use technology function more as *instructional designers* than lesson planners. This is especially true when they seek to incorporate computer-mediated innovations, such as telecomputing tools, into existing curriculums. If telecomputing tools' most powerful attributes (Clark 1983) are to be exploited, teachers must incorporate new techniques into new models of teaching and learning.

How Telecomputing Tools Differ From Other Tools

The process by which teachers either adopt or reject telecomputing tools is one example of the diffusion of innovations. Everett Rogers is a leading expert on the special nature of the processes that occur when members of a social system—like the faculty, staff, and parents at a school—adopt communications innovations, like Internet tools. Rogers (1995, p. 21) defines innovation adoption as "a decision to make full use of an innovation as the best course of action available." It is important to note that adoption of telecomputing tools implies regular and continuing use; we know that teachers and students have truly adopted the innovation when telecomputing is part of general classroom routine.

Rogers' meta-analytic synthesis of communications studies (1986) revealed three ways in which the adoption of interactive communications innovations differs from similar processes with other new ideas or tools.

1. A *critical mass* of adopters must use the innovation to persuade potential adopters to do the same; "the usefulness of a new communication system increases for all adopters with each additional adopter" (Rogers 1986, p. 120). A large number of teachers will not use telecommunications networks until they see a noticeable community of educators online or know of online information resources designed specifically to support K-12 teaching and learning.

2. The *degree of use* of a communications innovation, not the decision to adopt it, is the variable that will signify the success of the diffusion effort. Teachers will continue to work with Internet tools and resources only if they use them regularly and frequently from the start.

3. New communication technologies are tools, which can be applied in many different ways and for different purposes. Therefore, adoption of these innovations is an active process that involves much *reinvention*, or "the degree to which an innovation is changed or modified by a user in the process of its adoption and implementation" (Rogers 1995, pp. 16–17). Teachers will continue to use telecomputing tools in the classroom only if they can successfully design instructional activities that employ those tools in unique, personalized ways.

The importance of reinvention must not be overlooked. Innovations that are more flexible have many possible applications (like telecommunications tools), and are shared via a decentralized network (like the Internet) are more likely to be reinvented than those that are less flexible or are diffused according to a centralized plan (Rogers 1986). Also, reinvention appears to be very important psychologically to those who adopt innovations (Rogers 1995).

Users must take the new tool and "make it their own" if regular use of the innovation is to continue. When helping teachers to learn to use telecomputing tools, we must anticipate, stimulate, and encourage their *reinvention* of telecomputing applications. One way to do this is to provide multidisciplinary and cross-grade structures as models for activity design. In this way, teachers can function more as instructional designers than lesson planners, creating customized—rather than adapted—telecomputing applications.

The Telecomputing Teacher as Instructional Designer

Working alone in their classrooms, most teachers are both the designers and the deliverers of instruction (Briggs 1977). This implies that teachers are expected to create learning activities for their students on an ongoing basis, selecting, adapting, and using instructional materials and activities according to the needs and styles of each unique group of students. The extent to which this design process is effective determines, in part, students' eventual learning success.

When new teaching and learning tools are offered to educators for possible adoption, what happens? Once the initial technical and procedural aspects are presented (preferably through hands-on experience), curriculum integration is addressed. This sequence is appropriate because powerful educational applications of new technological tools with unique media attributes (Clark 1983) cannot be conceived until potential adopters are aware of the full range of those attributes (Rogers 1995).

But what happens then? In many cases, teachers are presented with a plethora of application ideas, often in the form of lesson plans or project reports that are separated into groups by content area or grade level. They are then asked to choose from many different activities that were created to fit the needs and preferences of groups of students different from their own. Then they are asked to adapt these activities for use in their own classrooms. With no guidance in the design of powerful applications for new tools, it is no wonder that so few activities exploit the unique characteristics of educational innovations. It's also little wonder that so many activities using new tools seem similar to projects done with more traditional media. One example of this pattern is the early proliferation of one-to-one pen pal letters sent via electronic mail (Riel and Levin 1990).

To ensure the adoption and continued use of innovations, teachers must have opportunities to reinvent educational applications in the role of instructional designer. Why ask teachers and students to expend time and energy on new tools—and decision makers to expend limited resources—if the tools cannot be used in inventive and more advantageous ways? Instructional uses for new tools cannot be modeled solely on the structures of educational activities done with more traditional media. All but the most creative and innovative educators will need new models for activity design.

Instructional Design: A Models Approach

The work of Joyce and Weil (1972, 1986) and their advocates (e.g., Gunter, Estes, and Schwab 1990) suggests that teachers' planning for instruction is greatly facilitated if they take a models approach to instructional design. With this approach, teachers choose from a

4

variety of structures (e.g., direct instruction, synectics, inquiry, class discussion, or cooperative learning) the model that, given the needs and preferences of a particular group of students, will best help learners accomplish specified educational goals. An important assumption of this approach is that there is no one "best" model for any student, teacher, or group. Instead, a carefully selected, consciously applied variety of models—a "cafeteria of alternatives" (Joyce and Weil 1972, p. xiv)—will help to create optimal learning environments for students.

Much of what has been published about using models for instructional design addresses the type of teacher-student and student-student interaction, asking the teacher to design specific learning activities that are appropriate in a particular classroom environment. While this level of guidance may be sufficient for teachers who are using familiar instructional media, it probably is insufficient for the teacher who wants to use powerful new educational innovations.

Teachers must be provided models for the design of forward-thinking, cross-curricular, multilevel activities and projects if telecomputing tools are to be used meaningfully in K-12 curriculums. Strain (1986) characterizes this distinction as the difference between a general "curriculum plan" and a specific "instructional procedure" (p. 287). Using models to design educational activities—rather than replicating or adapting existing lesson plans—allows for the large amount of reinvention necessary to make long-term adoption of telecomputing probable in K-12 classrooms.

The more an educational innovation differs from tools used before, the more important it is to provide teachers with flexible models, or activity structures, for specific instructional procedures. In Chapter 3, I will share 18 such frameworks for educational telecomputing. Helping teachers to recognize and, more important, *use* these structures for instructional design is suggested as the primary focus of professional development opportunities that you will offer after teachers are comfortable with basic telecomputing applications such as electronic mail and Web surfing and searching.

I identified these 18 frameworks through an informal content analysis of hundreds of educational telecomputing activities that were shared by teachers via the Internet. Among these activities, three genres emerged:

- interpersonal exchange,
- information collection and analysis, and
- problem solving.

Interpersonal Exchange

The most popular type of educational telecomputing activity is one where individuals "talk" electronically to other individuals or groups, or groups "talk" to other groups. Many of these projects use electronic mail as the common context for exchange. Others use newsgroups, realtime chatting facilities, interactive video conferencing, or Internet bulletin boards for exchange.

Keypals. Probably the most commonly used telecomputing activity structure, keypals is similar to traditional pen pal activities. Many student-to-student keypal exchanges involve more managerial work than many teachers have time for. But group-to-group exchanges, especially those with a particular study emphasis, can evolve into fascinating cultural explorations without overwhelming teachers with the transfer and processing of electronic mail.

Keypal activities are perfect conduits for language study. Figures 1.1 and 1.2 contain the introductory message (and its translation) from a group of students who live near Paris and want to learn about classes from other parts of the world where students are studying computer use.

Global Classrooms. In this variation on the group-to-group keypals structure, two or more classrooms (located anywhere in the world) study a common topic together, sharing what they learn about that topic. For example, two U.S. literature classes in two different schools studied *The Glass Menagerie* together, discussing the play by electronic mail.

In a larger-scale effort to involve many classes with HIV/AIDS awareness, Rhea Smith from the Jenkins Middle School in Palatka, Florida, designed a month-long series of activities so that her students helped, in her words, "teachers, parents, and children to understand the dangers of the HIV/AIDS virus and formulate a plan to remain HIV/AIDS negative."[1] The plan included suggestions for discussion and action for each week of activities.

Electronic Appearances. Electronic mail, newsgroups, chats, video conferences, and

[1]Quoted material in similar contexts throughout the book comes from e-mail or Web pages.

Figure 1.1.
KEYPAL INTRODUCTORY MESSAGE IN FRENCH

BONJOUR

Nous sommes des élèves de quatrième technologique et avons entre treize et seize ans. ROMAIN ROLLAND est un collège mixte, situé à CLICHY SOUS BOIS, dans la banlieue de PARIS. Les élèves d'une classe technologique doivent travailler sur des projets en faisant beaucoup de technologie et d'informatique. Nous voulons communiquer avec vous, pour mieux vous connaître.

- De quelle classe êtes vous?
- Où se situé votre collège?
- Faites vous de la technologie?
- Travaillez vous le samedi matin, le mercredi?
- Quels sont vos loisirs préférés?

Nous voulons aussi communiquer avec vous pour que vous puisiez nous aider dans nos recherches sur le thème du jeu.

electronic bulletin boards also can "host" a special guest with whom students can communicate either asynchronously or in real-time. One such electronic event was held in Academy One on the National Public Telecomputing Network's Cleveland Freenet. Nobel Laureate Paul Berg had a "virtual visit" with high school students from many different states, provinces, and countries. Berg electronically supplied a picture of himself and a paper that he had written on gene splicing that students could use to help them prepare questions for the electronic meetings.

Figure 1.2.
KEYPAL INTRODUCTORY MESSAGE TRANSLATED INTO ENGLISH

HELLO

We are a group of pupils, aged from 13 to 16 in 4eme technologique. ROMAIN ROLLAND is a mixed school, located in CLICHY SOUS BOIS, in the suburbs of PARIS. In a technology class, pupils must develop projects related to technology and computing. We want to communicate with you, in order to know you better.

- What is your class?
- Where is your school located?
- Do you take technology courses?
- Do you work on Saturday morning? Wednesday?
- What are your favorite activities?

We also want to communicate with you to get information on the subject of games.

Telementoring. Subject-matter specialists from universities, business, government, or other schools can serve as electronic mentors to students who want to explore specific topics in an interactive format. For two semesters, undergraduate students at the Oranim Teachers College in Israel, for example, served as mentors on the subject of prejudice for high school students in England, Australia, the United States, Ireland, and Israel. A "matching service" called the Electronic Emissary (http://www.tapr.org/emissary/)—sponsored by the Texas Center for Educational Technology, the University of Texas at Austin, and the J.C. Penney Corporation—helps volunteer subject-matter experts from all over the world link up with teachers and their classes, structure a telementoring project, and share what they learn together through electronic mail, chats, and CU-SeeMe video conferencing.

Question-and-Answer Activities. In the fall of 1994, the U.S. Geological Survey made an exciting new service available to Internet users. "Ask-A-Geologist" (http://walrus.wr.usgs.gov/docs/ask-a-ge.html), coordinated by Rex Sanders of the USGS Branch of Pacific Marine Geology, offers K-12 students the opportunity to submit questions to be answered by professional geologists. Such Q-and-A services allow students and teachers to quickly obtain answers they could not locate otherwise and when a longer-term correspondence is not required or desired.

Impersonations. Impersonation projects are those in which participants communicate with one another in character. In several of the electronic pavilions on Virginia's PEN (http://pen.k12.va.us/Anthology/Pav/), for example, students correspond with professors or graduate students posing as well-known historical figures, such as Thomas Jefferson, Woodrow Wilson, or William Shakespeare. In Characters Online, an Internet-based project sponsored by the Nebraska State Department of Education and the University of Nebraska at Omaha, undergraduate preservice teachers used electronic mail to communicate as the main characters from books that students in elementary classes in eastern Nebraska were reading with their teachers.

Students also can write messages or public postings in character for other students to read. In the California Missions project, coordinated by Nancy Sutherland from the FrEdMail Network, 21 4th grade classes in California (one for each of the 21 California missions) wrote and shared fictitious journal entries that described the lives and aspirations of people who participated in the missions in the early and middle 19th century.

Information Collection and Analysis

Some of the most successful educational telecomputing activities involve students who collect, compile, and compare different types of interesting information.

Information Exchanges. There are many examples of thematically related information exchanges that have been used as popular telecomputing activities. Students and their teachers from all around the globe have collected jokes, proverbs, folktales, directions for playing folk games, agricultural information, biome data, water usage information, recycling practices, personal health information, and culture-specific holiday descriptions, to name just a few.

This type of activity can involve many classes without becoming an overwhelming management task for teachers, and it is a particularly powerful telecommunications application because children become both the creators and consumers of the information that they exchange.

Database Creation. Some information collection projects involve not only collecting but also organizing information into databases that project participants and others can use for study. One such project was a statewide

exploration of Texas history from 1830 to 1900. The documents that resulted from students' research were added to an Internet-accessible Gopher and then used in further research and synthesis by more students.

Electronic Publishing. Another type of information collection and analysis is electronic publishing of a common document, such as a newspaper, poem, or literary magazine. In the Global SchoolNet's yearly Newsday project, (http://www.gsn.org/project/newsday/) teachers and students publish different newspapers locally, but take many of the stories for those local publications from a "newswire" shared electronically among all participating sites. The stories posted to this newswire are, of course, researched and written by students from schools in different cities, states, and countries. They all experience a realistic simulation of how many local newspapers are created and published.

Telefieldtrips. Organizers for the Global SchoolNet Foundation encourage Internet-connected teachers and students to share observations and experiences made during local field trips to museums, historical sites, parks, and zoos with teachers and students from other cities, states, and countries. The Global SchoolNet once maintained a monthly schedule of fieldtrip information posted by schools throughout the Internet and distributed it to interested teachers. They could then contact those scheduled to take fieldtrips that might yield information pertinent to their own curriculums. Electronic fieldtrips also can be taken and shared without anyone leaving the classroom, as students exchange information about the places where they live.

7

8

Experts on expeditions also share information on the Internet. The International Arctic Project, a "multi-national expedition across the Arctic Ocean by dogsled and canoe," was described and updated by teachers involved with the World School for Adventure Learning through the Kidsphere electronic mailing list. During an expedition, participating classes received weekly, detailed descriptions of the progress of two explorers from the United Kingdom: what they experienced and the challenges that they faced. When the successful explorers visited the United Nations for a heroes' welcoming party, they found a wall of electronic mail waiting for them from children all over the world who had vicariously experienced their expedition.

Pooled Data Analysis. Information exchanges are particularly powerful when data are collected at multiple sites, then combined for numeric or pattern analysis. The simplest of these types of activities involves students electronically issuing a survey, collecting the responses, analyzing the results, and reporting their findings to all participants. Pooled data projects also have included:

• Water acidity projects in which rain or stream water is collected at different points along a common waterway, tested for acidity, then examined for patterns over time and distance.

• The Global Grocery List project (http://www.landmark-project.com/ggl.html), coordinated by David Warlick from North Carolina, in which students compare prices of 14 standard items (such as rice, sugar, eggs, and peanut butter). They then attempt to deduce reasons for price differences.

• The Column Count project, coordinated by Joyce Rudowski, a teacher at the Cincinnati Country Day School, in which students from different cities measured the number of inches devoted to newspaper stories on different topics, then compared space allocations across participating sites.

• The Tele-Olympics, coordinated by Linda Delzeit from the Cleveland Freenet, in which students at many different schools conducted Olympic-style athletic events, then submitted the statistics generated to determine the winners for each "virtual event."

These types of projects hold much promise for involving students in large-scale research efforts that use mathematics to answer complex and interesting questions.

Problem Solving

Problem solving can take on exciting new dimensions in telecomputing environments. Activities can be either competitive or collaborative.

Information Searches. In this type of online activity, students are provided with clues and must use reference sources (electronic and/or paper-based) to solve problems. For example, Tom Clauset of Winston-Salem, North Carolina, developed the GeoGame (http://www.gsn.org/project/gg/). Each of many participating groups of students provides the same 10 pieces of information about its school's location (i.e., latitude, time zone, population, direction from capital city). The coordinators of the game then scramble the city names, and all groups use reference materials such as maps, atlases, books, and Web pages to match the cities with the sets of information. The winning class is the one that correctly identifies the most participating sites.

Peer Feedback Activities. Students in Trevor Owen's English classes in Toronto, Ontario, Canada, regularly posted the poems that they had written to newsgroups sponsored by Simon Fraser University so that other students in Canada could offer feedback in an electronic version of process writing sessions. Owen was also able to enlist the assistance of professional writers, such as the poet Lionel Kearns, to offer constructive criticism and to receive some of the same from students in response to pieces in progress. The project has now grown to encompass several different activity structures and is called Writers in Electronic Residence (http://www.edu.yorku.ca/wierhome/).

Parallel Problem Solving. With this activity structure, a similar problem is presented to students in several locations, which they solve at each site. Then they share their problem-solving methods electronically. For example, Carmela Federico of New York City presented an architectural challenge online as in Figure 1.3.

Sequential Creations. Expressive problem solving can be experienced with many students working on the same piece, rather than the same collection. Students on the FrEdMail network, for example, collaboratively created a "Global Peace Poem" (conceived and coordinated by Yvonne Andres and Mary Jacks) that circled the globe several times. Each class of students in each location added a stanza after reading the verses that other students created.

Figure 1.3.
AN ONLINE ARCHITECTURAL CHALLENGE

What's the tallest structure you can build out of 3/4" wide popsicle sticks that can:
• Support a Grade A Large egg and
• Withstand the Big Bad Wolf Test (the biggest lungs in the room blow on it as long and hard as possible; if the structure stands, it passes)?

We at the Playing to Win Saturday Science Project challenge you to come up with interesting, strong structures to perform this engineering feat!

• Use only Elmer's Glue for adhesive.
• Egg must be hard-boiled, with the shell intact.

9

Telepresent Problem Solving. Virtual gatherings bring together participants from different geographic locations and time zones in real time to either participate in a computer-mediated meeting or, without direct electronic contact, do similar activities at different project sites. Students using the KIDCLUB Internet Relay Chat (IRC) channel can participate on most Saturdays, for example, in discussions organized by Patti Weeg (pweeg@shore.net.com). On one Saturday, students chatted about what they would do "if they were in charge of the school." On another Saturday, students in the United Kingdom held a 24-hour telecommunications vigil to help other students worldwide understand and ease difficulties encountered by Lebanese children.

Simulations. Online simulations are the

10

telecomputing projects that require the most coordination and maintenance, but the depth of learning possible and the amount of student engagement often convinces teachers to spend the additional time and effort necessary to make them work. A notable example of a successful online simulation was Centennial Launches, sponsored by the Cleveland Freenet's Academy One, which was described in an electronic newsletter (fig. 1.4).

Figure 1.4.
CENTENNIAL LAUNCHES: SIMULATED SPACE SHUTTLE PROGRAM

At the core of these launches is a permanent full-scale mock-up of a space shuttle (called the "Centennial") complete with "Mission Control," which is located at University School in Shaker Heights, Ohio (Cleveland area). Schools around the world take various roles in each simulated space shuttle mission. These could include being another shuttle (doing a docking maneuver), secondary mission control, alternate landing sites (weather stations), solar disturbance observatories, and so forth.

Coordination and communications between the shuttle's mission control and other schools will be conducted through distributed conferences on the individual NPTN [National Public Telecomputing Network] systems. Electronic mail is sent back and forth, hourly reports are posted, even realtime electronic chats can occur between mission control, astronauts, and supporting units.

Social Action Projects. The Internet can serve as a context for "humanitarian, multicultural, action-oriented telecommunications projects" that involve the future leaders of our planet: children. The PLANET Project (People Linking Across Networks), one of many social action efforts sponsored by I*EARN (http://www.iearn.org/iearn/), involved representatives from a consortium of large, Internet-accessible educational networks. These participants worked together to create collaborative, meaningful social action projects in which children had primary responsibility for learning about and helping to tackle global issues such as hunger, violence, environmental pollution, and disease.

During the first months of operation, PLANET participants wrote petitions to the United Nations to protest conditions in Yugoslavia, brainstormed ideas about how to address starvation and political unrest in Somalia, and planned for and carried out fundraising efforts to help purchase "rope pumps for villages in Nicaragua that do not have access to clean water."

Additional information about and examples of all of the above structures can be found both in Chapter 3 of this book and on the World Wide Web at http://www.ed.uiuc.edu/Activity-Structures/.

What Research Reveals About Teachers and Innovations

The ideas behind the sample curriculum-infused telecollaborative activities presented in Chapter 1 are simple, yet powerful. Their power rests in the interconnectedness that participants experience when communicating across what were once geographic and temporal boundaries to collectively realize meaningful, shared goals. This *interconnectedness*—and the energy, enthusiasm, commitment, and patience of the teachers and students who help to bring these plans to life—are probably the keys to their inspiring success. For successes like these to proliferate in K–12 settings, effective structures for curriculum-based telecomputing activity design and implementation must be provided. But to *whom* should they be presented, and when? Strategic selection of members of a social system, such as a school or school district, and the manner and order in which they are offered workshop opportunities, can also assist diffusion efforts.

Have you ever wondered why certain teachers decide to use telecommunications tools sooner than others? Have you noticed that the teachers who first volunteer to attend

12

a workshop or demonstration are quite different from those who volunteer much later? At times, do you feel as if you can predict certain teachers' responses when you offer to help them learn about something, like the use of telecomputing tools?

If so, you may be seeing patterns that have been documented in more than 30 years of research. These studies explore how people in communities react, over time, to the introduction of new tools and the new ideas that often accompany them. These are important issues to consider when introducing telecomputing to teachers. You can enhance your diffusion efforts by strategically selecting educators to receive training and by specifically choosing how and when to offer them workshop opportunities.

The Research Base

Everett Rogers has led the research tradition that teaches us about who adopts innovations, when they do so in comparison to their peers, and what conditions accompany changes in their behavior. He has spent much of his career exploring the connections between communication and innovation (1995, 1986). Rogers has shown that information about new tools, including telecommunications applications, travels by interpersonal connections. Each person's decision about whether to use a new tool regularly (in other words, to adopt it) is more dependent upon who shares the news of the tool than upon how well the tool might actually assist them.

Rogers and his colleagues explain that many peers do not trust the opinions of the most innovative members of any social system. Therefore, when these "change agents" adopt innovations like telecomputing tools, they do little to influence most others to also try the new tools. This means, for example, that the very first educators to create Web pages often will not be emulated by fellow faculty members. As a matter of fact, most of the community may perceive this innovative behavior as abnormal.

Rogers discovered that *opinion leaders* in social systems can help others become receptive to adopting an innovation. Opinion leaders are people to whom others look for information and advice about new ideas, tools, and techniques. Their positions of authority are rarely official or formal, but they are the teachers whose perspectives are sought out by others most frequently and consistently.

Though opinion leaders are often technically competent, they are much more socially accessible than teachers who adopt an innovation first. More important, opinion leaders conform to the system's norms much more than change agents do. In other words, they interact frequently with many members of the faculty, they are well respected, and most colleagues regard them as "normal." Thus, Rogers points out that if the social norms of the community support change, opinion leaders will be more innovative than if the social system resists change. At this point, it may be easy for you to see how groups of teachers resistant to change may be exceedingly difficult to convince to try new tools or techniques.

If opinion leaders will be most effective in persuading colleagues to explore and use tele-computing tools, how can you identify who they are? Rogers offers the following characteristics (Rogers 1995, pp. 293–304).

• Opinion leaders are more exposed to all forms of communication outside the social system (including mass media) and therefore are more cosmopolitan.

• They have somewhat higher social status outside the school community than other members of the social system.

• They have unique and influential positions within the system's communications networks. They are at the hubs of the system's interpersonal webs.

• They are more innovative when compared with the system's norms. But they can't be too much like change agents if their peers are to trust and emulate them.

This research implies that access to tele-computing resources and support for their use in the forms of training, ongoing assistance, funding, and—most important—*time* should be concentrated upon those opinion leaders who are most willing to explore professional development about and instructional use of Internet tools. We can infer from Rogers' work that as these opinion leaders become comfortable and competent in cyberspace, they will, by their example, personally influence many colleagues who are reticent to explore new uses for new classroom tools. This grassroots pattern of diffusion may seem slower and less comprehensive than traditional top-down mandates, but it is, overall, a more effective plan because it complements the nat-

ural ways in which new tools are adopted by members of social systems.

The Predictable Chronology of Adoption

One of the most remarkable aspects of diffusion research is that no matter what kind of social system or what type of innovation was studied, similar proportions of people adopted or rejected innovations according to a fairly predictable chronology. Though the groups differ, members of each group share similar characteristics.

Innovators

The first 2–3 percent of a social system to adopt a new tool, idea, or technique are the innovators (with respect to a particular innovation, rather than in general). Rogers describes innovators as being "venturesome," with control of substantial resources. They often can easily understand and apply technical knowledge, and they form friendships and communicate most frequently with other innovators. They usually have many more contacts outside their local social systems than others. Do you see why telecollaborative tools, in particular, can support innovators quite well?

Innovators can tolerate a large amount of uncertainty about an innovation without being discouraged from using it, and they are therefore willing to accept an occasional setback in the acclimation process. Rogers says that they exhibit a desire to try ideas that are rash, risky, or daring when compared to what most of the other members of the social system are willing

14

to do. They may not be understood or respected by the majority of their contemporaries. They also are quite self-motivated to try things that they believe will provide what Rogers calls "relative advantage," or increased benefit, when compared with use of an existing tool, idea, or technique. Innovators often will persist in their attempts to secure consistent access to the innovation, despite almost insurmountable odds. Their point of reference is the future.

Early Adopters

The next 13–14 percent of the members of a social system to embrace an innovation are known as early adopters. In contrast to innovators, early adopters are generally well-respected by their peers. They have more of a local orientation than innovators, whose perspectives are often quite cosmopolitan and global. Early adopters are more integrated into the social system than innovators are; they are seen as the "teachers to check with" when a new approach is being considered. Early adopters are known to others in the social system for successful but discrete use of new tools, methods, or ideas, and, as such, they often serve as role models. Whereas innovators may be seen as "a breed apart," early adopters are thought to be talented but still "one of the folks."

Do you have some ideas about who might be the innovators and the early adopters in the social system in which you work? If not, please read over these characteristics again and form some hypotheses. Early adopters and innovators will be your greatest allies in your efforts to diffuse telecommunications innovations.

Early Majority

There is a big difference between early adopters and early majority members, who comprise the next 33–34 percent of the system to adopt an innovation. Early majority members are known for their high frequency of interaction with their colleagues. Unlike innovators and early adopters, they often do not hold leadership positions within the social system, either officially or unofficially. Their primary role is to provide connections between and among the different interpersonal networks that function within the social system. It takes them much longer to decide to try a new tool, technique, or idea than early adopters and innovators. Rogers says that early majority members "follow with deliberate willingness" (Rogers 1995, p. 265). Their decision process is often more careful, conscious, and cautious than peers who adopted an innovation earlier.

Once a new idea has caught on among early majority members, it spreads rather quickly, mostly because of their predisposition to interaction with others. Critical mass is reached during the adoption process among this particular group's members. Rogers (1986) points out that a critical mass of users is especially important for telecommunications innovations because telecomputing is interactive, and telecomputing tools are truly adopted only when members of the social system continue to use them in ways that are self-tailored, or reinvented, to meet professional and personal needs.

Late Majority

Members of the late majority in a social system make up the next 33–34 percent. These folks are quite skeptical of new ideas, methods, and tools, making them much more cautious about trying an innovation than any of the groups already discussed. They also have relatively scarce classroom resources, which adds to their difficulties in using computer-mediated tools in many schools in which computer and Internet accessibility are meager.

Rogers tells us that late majority members often will adopt an innovation only out of economic necessity or in response to strong peer pressure. For late majority folks to adopt an innovation, most of the uncertainty about it must have already been removed, and the norms for behavior and belief in the social system must already favor its adoption.

You may be thinking that late majority members are tough people to convince to try a new idea, tool, or technique. Perhaps so, but there's a remaining group that is even more challenging in this regard.

Laggards

Did you chuckle when you read the name that Rogers has given to this group? Did synonyms like "dinosaurs," "fossils," or "neo-Luddites" occur to you? Actually, Rogers warns us against seeing the last 15–16 percent of the social system negatively or as somehow worthy of blame. Laggards are the most traditional of all of the members of the social system. They are extremely cautious in exploring new ideas, tools, and techniques, and they often have few resources to support their doing so. Their point of reference is the past. Therefore, they serve an important function in the social system: They remember its history and provide its continuity.

While innovators are the most globally oriented of all of the social system members, laggards are the most localized. Yet, laggards and innovators are quite similar in that they most frequently interact with others very similar to themselves, and they can be loners in professional or personal contexts. Laggards are very suspicious of innovations and change agents. They adopt an innovation a very long time after they have become aware of it, and usually only when survival within the social system absolutely demands this change.

Rogers says that most of us who help diffuse innovations choose to work first with those folks who are more likely to adopt. He reminds us that we instead could decide to concentrate our early efforts on the least innovative in a social system—laggards and late majority members—in an effort to close the gap between those who have resources and those who do not. Remember that earlier adopters are usually higher in general social and economic status and have control of significantly more school-based resources than later adopters. This approach may be more challenging, but in the long run it may be better suited to certain contexts, especially when equity issues are an important concern within the social system.

How Can You Put This Knowledge Into Action?

Perhaps by now you are starting to think about different ways in which you can approach members of these five different groups in your own school or district. Following are some suggestions for working with each group, though every social system is unique and not all of these techniques will be equally effective in every context. In most cases, you will first be addressing innovators' needs, then adding early majority members to your target population, and so on, as adoption of telecomputing innovations spreads throughout your social system.

Innovators

Stay out of their way! Keep them supplied with as many resources as possible: hardware, software, connectivity, individualized instruction, interpersonal connections, administrative permission, project calls for participation, guidelines for grant proposals, and keys to the computer lab. Try to shield them from bureaucratic red tape, others' jealousy, and parental ire. Help them to find other innovators, both inside the local system and beyond, with whom they can explore innovation applications. Don't force or coerce them to teach others, especially those who are less innovative in their approaches.

Early Adopters

Make their successes public, but be careful to allow them to make adoption decisions at their own pace. Don't push! Instead, offer again and again to help them explore rich, well-grounded, high-quality applications of innovations. For teachers, this means exposing them to curriculum-based, educationally sound learning activities that are clearly linked to what they already do in their classrooms. Remember that more than any other group, these educators will "sell" the innovation for you to their peers. Don't rush them in doing so. They will figure out powerful, persuasive uses and reasons for adoption if you support and encourage their work.

Early Majority

Make good use of this group's relatively large size and even more so its preference for interaction with other educators. Encourage collaborative explorations and applications of new tools, ideas, and techniques. (Telecollaborative tools like electronic mail, chatting services, and bulletin boards should be quite appealing to many in this group.) Be patient! These people will take much longer to make adoption decisions than the groups that preceded them, but after they do so, they will apply the tools consciously, confidently, and conspicuously. Once they begin to embrace the innovation, the overall rate of diffusion in the social system will quicken. Be ready to move faster once this occurs.

Late Majority

You probably won't have to work as hard to get these folks to try a new idea, tool, or technique. Said another way, no matter how hard you try, these folks probably won't adopt the innovation until its use is common in the social system. That said, why set unrealistic expectations for yourself? The more that you can publicize the use of an innovation as "normal" and "expected," the better chance you will have in winning over these cautious folks. Don't force them, embarrass them, or get frustrated with them. More important, make sure that they have the resources that they believe are necessary to consider adoption. Keep offering opportunities; don't be deterred by lack of response. One day they will accept.

Laggards

Some educational technologists suggest, tongue in cheek, that the best strategy to use with laggards is to wait until they retire. Instead, I suggest that you use techniques similar to those offered for late majority members—but with even more patience and acceptance. Once use of the innovation is perceived by most as being "the way that we do things here," the laggards will come along, albeit reluctantly and quietly. Keep their secret for and with them. It's not remarkable that they finally relented. Use of the innovation has now become the overwhelming behavioral norm.

A Few Caveats

Rogers tells us that there are some social systems for which innovation adoption does not proceed according to these predictable patterns. If that is apparent in your context, try to figure out why this difference is occurring. Identifying possible causes for uncharacteristic patterns will help you to know how best to encourage diffusion under a different set of conditions.

Also, keep in mind another remarkably consistent finding of diffusion research. No matter what the nature of the social system, approximately 10 percent of all of the users of a telecomputing system generate approximately 50 percent of all of the traffic on the system (Rogers 1986). Isn't that amazing? That means that the other 90 percent of the users contribute the other 50 percent of the use. So, expect everyone to use the tools, ideas, and resources that you have so carefully and persistently promoted very differently. As educators, we try our best to recognize, respect, and accommodate the different needs, interests, and preferences of students. When teachers are the students, we should proceed similarly.

Rogers reminds us that the distribution of innovators into these five categories is innovation-specific, and only occurs in these proportions if the innovation is eventually adopted by everyone. Many innovation diffusion efforts fail. Reasons can range from the political to the personal to the procedural (1995, pp. 260–261).

Formats for Professional Development

Your telecomputing workshops will be more effective overall if you *offer* them, rather than *require* them, and if you provide maximum support first to a smaller number of volunteer participants who are opinion leaders. Those folks will naturally spread the word through their own communications channels, and they can help you attract additional participants later. The key idea in this plan is that true change in perspective, and therefore practice, comes only as a result of a conscious, self-initiated, and willing decision by each practitioner. That kind of change cannot be mandated but certainly can be catalyzed, energized, and supported. Your role, then, is to facilitate more than deliver, encourage instead of mandate, assist rather than coerce.

To use the Internet for both professional development and instructional purposes requires constant accommodation to rapid change, successful use of varied interfaces, and, most important, tolerance for ambiguity. These problem-solving skills cannot be taught directly; rather, their development can be assisted through relevant instruction in appropriate formats to willing participants. This instruction usually takes one of eight forms, as described below.

Independent Learning

Many teachers who travel in cyberspace have learned to use telecomputing resources independently, with little assistance. This is probably the most time-consuming and frustrating way to learn, due to the highly ambiguous and changing nature of the Internet and the cumbersome procedures necessary to navigate in cyberspace.

Independent Learning with Remote Assistance

Most teachers who presently use Internet tools have learned to do so by applying patience, persistence, and good problem-solving skills both independently and with assistance from more experienced colleagues.

Because comparatively few teachers have classroom access to the Internet, this is the most prevalent, but not necessarily the most efficient, model for learning to use telecomputing tools. It is one best suited to innovators, who makeup only 2 to 3 percent of the population of any social system.

One-to-One Coaching

Some teachers are lucky enough to work or live near a more experienced "Internaut" who is willing to provide informal, individualized telecomputing training. As communities of telecomputing teachers are formed within existing social systems, this very effective model for learning to use Internet tools will become more commonplace. It is especially effective for early adopters and early majority members because of their preferences for interpersonal exchanges of information and opinion.

Large-Group Demonstration with Independent Practice

In the early stages of work with telecomputing innovations, a school or district usually offers demonstrations of Internet resources and tools to large groups of teachers and administrators. Unfortunately, these "awareness sessions" rarely communicate the significant challenge involved with independently learning to access and use telecomputing resources. Therefore, this model is more effective in coaxing teachers to decide to adopt an innovation and in marshaling support from decision makers. It's not nearly as useful for helping anyone to truly use Internet resources.

Large-Group Demonstration with Assisted Practice

This format improves upon the previous idea in that it can be effective both in convincing decision makers to provide for the infusion of telecomputing tools and in helping teachers to use the provisions once they are in place. However, it is generally not as successful in terms of diffusion as are the following three formats.

Hands-On Lab, Intensive Schedule

It is probably no surprise that one of the most effective models for telecomputing training is one where teachers use computer-mediated tools in a hands-on, collaborative context in which brief demonstrations are followed immediately by assisted exploration in many situations and for many purposes. Teachers' schedules make the time for such hands-on experiences quite limited, though.

An intensive schedule (i.e., several half-day or full-day sessions on weekends) is most often used for hands-on training. But due to the overwhelming amount of information available on the Internet and the multiple skills necessary to master effective access to and use of that information, this may not be the best training model for teachers. Professional development that "dumps" too much information on teachers often doesn't ensure retention and use of the skills and ideas introduced.

Hands-On Lab, Paced Schedule

Spreading hands-on experiences evenly over several months of Internet work is prefer-able to planning labs on an intensive schedule. This approach is successful mostly because it allows teachers to practice the skills that they learned independently or with individualized assistance before they encounter the next new skill or resource type. It is admittedly difficult, though, to assure that the between-meetings work gets done, given the many professional and personal demands upon teachers' time. Participants must understand and commit to such practice before they agree to participate in training sessions.

Hands-On Lab, Paced Schedule, with Structured Online Activities

Although this model takes the most effort for telecomputing trainers, it is probably the most effective overall. Online communities of networked teachers will emerge if highly interactive, hands-on sessions offered at regular intervals in lab settings are supplemented by structured, motivating, between-session online activities—and if teachers feel responsible for these activities and are committed to completing them. Whether or not these communities continue to function after training (either intact or in expanded forms) depends upon the extent to which individual participants have truly adopted telecomputing innovations and see themselves as contributing members of the community. The success of this particular professional development model, in terms of helping teachers to develop transferable and longitudinal telecomputing skills, attests to the current popularity of the online course.

19

Tools and Their Uses

It is important to remember that different conditions of access to, purposes for, and support of telecomputing tools and resources will greatly affect your choices of which training models are the most appropriate, time-effective, and cost-efficient for your school or district. The descriptions just discussed are offered as an array of possibilities, rather than a hierarchy of recommendations. The list also is unfinished. New models will undoubtedly emerge as increasing numbers of teachers and students have access to and learn to use the Internet.

Please note that the formats listed here can be interpreted as if they emphasize learning to use different types of Internet tools and resources. However, the primary focus of this book centers on helping teachers to learn to design powerful telecomputing activities that will help students accomplish curriculum-based learning goals. This book does not advise how to teach teachers to use telecommunications tools; it aims to show how teachers can use those tools in curriculum-related ways.

In my experience conducting workshops on this topic, the most effective session structure focusing on design is face-to-face and collaborative, using both large-group and small-group presentations and cooperative learning activities. Also, if we want teachers to concentrate upon curriculum-based activity design, it is best *not* to have online resources accessible to them for unstructured, hands-on use during the majority of professional development sessions. "Surfing" during a workshop is a powerful distraction to even the most motivated professional, and putting this activity on the agenda can be interpreted as a focus upon the *tools* and the information that they can yield, rather than how *use* of the tools can serve students' curriculum-based learning goals. The context in and conditions under which you work, though, will dictate the content, format, and style most appropriate for meeting the needs and addressing the interests of the teachers whom you will teach to design curriculum-based educational telecomputing activities.

Eighteen Activity Structures for Telecomputing Projects

Internet accounts give users access to an almost inconceivable amount and variety of online information. Within the vast array of possible connections on the Internet, there are basically two ways to share information online: *among people* and *between people and remotely located machines*.

Internetworked computers can house publicly accessible databases, multimedia documents with hypertextual links, file archives, and virtual environments. I call these *informational resources*. When using an informational resource, you are actually interacting with a computer program, using it to help you to locate and collect information. Computers on the Internet can also house user accounts, with which accountholders can communicate either privately or publicly with other users, sharing information person-to-person. The tools that allow us to make such interpersonal connections, both asynchronously and in real-time, can be seen as *interpersonal resources*.

Both informational and interpersonal resources can be used to help students explore curriculum-related topics in K-12 classrooms. In the next section, I will review and expand upon the six types of *interpersonal exchanges*, or educational telecomputing activities introduced in Chapter 1 that incorporate use of interpersonal resources. This section and the two that follow feature examples of three different general classes of educational telecomputing activities: *interpersonal exchange*, *information collection and analysis*, and *problem solving*. Each genre includes at least five different *activity structure*s, and each is described below with at least one sample activity that has been classroom tested and shared by telecomputing teachers.

When teachers are offered activity structures instead of a potpourri of lesson plans, they are empowered to design effective telecomputing experiences for their students that are curriculum-based and adapted to suit particular learning needs and preferences.

Interpersonal Exchange

Interpersonal exchanges are among the most popular educational telecomputing activities. With these types of projects, students "talk" electronically with other students, individuals "talk" to groups, or groups "talk" with other groups. Many of these projects use e-mail as the common context for exchange. Others use newsgroups, chats, interactive video connections, and bulletin boards.

Keypals

Keypal projects were the first educational telecomputing activities to be tested online. When an online activity is organized using this structure, individual students in two or more locations are matched with one another so that they can communicate using e-mail.

For example, students at Burleson High School in Texas communicated with students from South Africa, Norway, Finland, Denmark, Peru, Russia, Estonia, Chile, Mexico, England, Iceland, Germany, and Canada. They exchanged information about their experiences in their different countries as part of a project called The World at Our Fingertips. Their teacher, Brenda Yowell, arranged for these exchanges by posting a message to the KIDLINK discussion list (http://www.kidlink.org/).

Diane Eisner of Lexington, Massachusetts, similarly arranged for her 85 7th grade students to discuss the books *I Am Rosemarie* and *The Cay* with "electronic literature partners" via electronic mail and discussions on IRC (Internet Relay Chat).

"Town twinning" projects match students from towns with the same names in different countries. This kind of project also can be conducted with the keypal activity structure. For example, students from Mano Talaiver's classes in Richmond, Virginia, communicated with Mike Burleigh's students from Richmond-on-Thames in the United Kingdom. First they answered the four questions that all participants on the KIDPROJ (http://www.kidlink.org/KIDPROJ/) discussion list must address:

• Who am I?
• What do I want to be when I grow up?
• How do I want the world to be better when I grow up?
• What can I do now to make this happen?
Melanie Golding, an English teacher from

a high school in northern New York, structured a six-week keypal project in which her 14- to 17-year-old students exchanged information about their families, town histories, schools, local geography and history, local and federal governments, and holiday customs. The educational goals for keypal projects in general are well stated in Figure 3.1, which is an excerpt from the message that Melanie posted to announce the availability of this Getting to Know You project.

Figure 3.1.
EDUCATIONAL GOALS OF THE GETTING TO KNOW YOU PROJECT

I hope that my students are able to connect with students from France, Germany, or Israel because they have studied these countries this year in their history classes. My intention is to foster communication, technology, and cultural awareness. This can happen by merely letting the children talk. We can start this process by having the children write individually to one another.

Unfortunately, student-to-student keypal exchanges often involve more managerial work than many teachers have time to contribute. Group-to-group exchanges, especially those with a particular study emphasis, can evolve into fascinating explorations without overwhelming teachers with the processing of multiple e-mail messages sent to and from a single account. Such "global classroom" activities are presented in the next section.

Global Classrooms

Using this activity structure, two or more groups of students (located anywhere in the world, of course) study a common topic together, sharing what they learn about that theme during a specific time period. This has become one of the most popular types of educational telecomputing projects.

For example, students from Barrow, Alaska—along with their teacher, Maryann Holmquist—posted the message in Figure 3.2 to initiate a simple, fascinating global classroom project.

Figure 3.2.
A MESSAGE FROM STUDENTS IN ALASKA

Greetings from Barrow, Alaska, USA. It is pretty cold in the Arctic. We live in a desert but tomorrow (Nov. 18) when the sun dips below the horizon like a seal we will not see it again for 65 days. Sunrise is at 12:37 p.m. and it sets at 1:46 p.m. for a total of 1 hour, 9 minutes of day. The horizon will be a fiery orange. We will continue to ride on snowmobiles and go sliding and when we get cold we'll go inside.

Write to us and tell us something about the sun from where you live on this planet. How much sunlight do you get? Do you have a favorite sunset you remember?

—From the Kids at Ipalook School

Figure 3.3 shows a message from students in Caribou, Maine. They organized a project through which several groups could explore similar cultural roots.

Figure 3.3.
COMPARING CULTURES AND LIFESTYLES

We are grade 8 students from Caribou, Maine, who have Acadian roots (French), and we want to compare our cultures and lifestyles with the Louisiana Cajuns. Is there anyone out there who may know of schools or individuals in the Lafayette, Breaux Bridge, Broussard, and Iberia regions of Louisiana who have electronic mail capabilities with access to Internet? We are excited about this project and want to start as soon as possible. Please spread the word. :-)

—Paula Robertson
Ruth Dionne

Eight-year-old students from New Zealand studied the subject of villages—including the Global Village—by asking students worldwide to answer the questions in Figure 3.4.

Figure 3.5 shows how other New Zealand students, with the help of their teacher Sue Graham, answered the questions in Figure 3.4.

Please note that global classroom projects often are more topically focused than keypal projects. Also, they involve groups of students communicating with one another rather than individual students. In one activity, for example, technology specialist Enola Boyd from Amarillo, Texas, organized a collaborative exploration of nuclear facilities among a half-dozen upper elementary classes. In Boyd's

words, participating students "studied the functions and impacts of nuclear facilities on their surrounding communities."

Figure 3.4.
QUESTIONS FROM NEW ZEALAND STUDENTS

1. What do you think a village is?
2. Could your area be called a village? If not, how do you describe your area?
3. List some features of your village. (We're looking for similarities and differences here.)
4. Do you know of any other kinds of villages?
5. Do you think our class could be part of The Global Village?

Here's a question in case none of the above questions appeals!

6. What do you think the Global Village means?

While some global classroom projects are simple and short-lived, others are quite complex and can involve students for one or more school semesters. The Desert and Desertification project (http://environment.negev.k12.il/desert/desert.htm) was coordinated by Hannah Sivan, David Lloyd, and Oded Bar from Sde Boker, Israel. This yearlong, four-stage interdisciplinary project worked with students from around the world who were interested in studying deserts in the past, present, and future. It included a rich array of activities, involving participants in discussion, online and offline data collection and organization, sound and image collection and transmission, film viewing, interviews with subject-matter experts, literary analysis, desert field-trips, simulations, roleplays, and environmental forecasting.

Figure 3.5.
NEW ZEALAND STUDENTS DESCRIBE THEIR VILLAGE

We think a village is a place where families live. It is a group of houses and shops close together.

We live in the city of Dunedin, New Zealand, which is halfway between the Equator and the South Pole, and we're the first country in the world to see the sunrise each day. Our shopping centre is called the Roslyn Village, which is on the top of the hill surrounded by very busy roads. We have lots of shops very close together. There are a number of old wooden villas, some big brick houses, some narrow steep streets, and not many open spaces.

The Maoris, who lived in NZ before the Europeans arrived, used to live in a fortified village called a "pa." This was usually on the top of a hill, with a fence to keep out enemies and a good view to see other tribes coming to attack.

We're not sure what The Global Village is, but we know that it has something to do with people living in our world.

What is your village like? Is your "village" like ours or is it different?

The S.S. Central America: A Shipwreck to Remember was a similarly rich and varied four-stage, interdisciplinary, yearlong project with historical and meteorological emphases. It was coordinated by Jamie Wilkerson of Rosewood Elementary School in Rock Hill, South Carolina. Groups of students from different schools electronically explored the voyage and sinking of a 272-foot wooden steamship along with the weather conditions that led to its demise. They worked in electronic consultation with members of the Columbus-America Discovery Group, the team of scientists and historians who were then working to salvage the Central America's history and treasures.

Electronic Appearances

Electronic mail, chat rooms, CU-SeeMe sites, newsgroups, and electronic bulletin boards also can "host" special guests with whom students can communicate. A series of such "electronic events" was held regularly in Academy One on the National Public Telecomputing Network (NPTN), coordinated by Linda Delzeit. One event connected students with authors of children's books, such as Sheri Cooper Sinykin, who wrote *The Buddy Trap*, *Slate Blues*, and *Next Thing to Strangers*. She answered students' previously submitted questions in a public conferencing area. Authors participating in these periodic virtual appearances also shared, according to Delzeit, "background information, a little about what they have written, and insights on the writing process."

The 50th Anniversary of D-Day, an historically focused electronic appearance activity, helped students to explore World War II by asking electronically for participants' memories. Figure 3.6 summarizes the project.

Figure 3.6.
THE 50TH ANNIVERSARY OF D-DAY PROJECT

The Department of Defense has a World War II Commemorative Community Program surrounding the 50th anniversary events. Fact Sheets from the DOD are posted on various facets of WW II. A special panel of WW II survivors are available for students to ask questions. Some memories have been posted from these survivors that make interesting reading and research. As part of the Commemorative Community Program you can sign up your community, school, and community computer system as Commemorative Communities. Each community that registers will receive a Commemorative Flag authorized to be flown on poles just below the State Flag, and each member of the committee will receive a special lapel pin.

NPTN also hosted a multinational Career Panel, which called upon a large number of adults in many different kinds of jobs to share details of their responsibilities, employers, work schedules, tools, and educational or professional preparation.

Electronic appearance projects usually allow students to communicate with local, national, or international experts for relatively short periods of time. When exchanges with these experts become more extended and an "electronic apprenticeship" forms, the activity structure can be called electronic mentoring, or telementoring.

Telementoring

Subject-matter specialists from universities, businesses, government, or other schools can serve as electronic mentors to students for ongoing exploration of specific topics of study in an interactive format. For example, a "matching service" called the Electronic Emissary, based at the University of Texas at Austin, helps teachers and their classes find volunteer subject-matter experts from all over the world, structure a telementoring project, and share what they learn together by communicating with electronic mail (http://www.tapr.org/emissary/).

Students also can serve as mentors to other students. Philip Sandberg's undergraduate geology students at the University of Illinois, Urbana-Champaign, served as mentors to K-12 teachers and students as part of their requirements for their History of Life course. In Figure 3.7, Sandberg describes the intent of the project.

Question-and-Answer Activities

In the fall of 1994, the U.S. Geological Survey (USGS) made an exciting new service available to Internet users. "Ask-A-Geologist" (http://walrus.wr.usgs.gov/docs/ask-a-ge.html), coordinated by Rex Sanders of the USGS Branch of Pacific Marine Geology, allows K-12 students to submit questions that are answered by professional geologists. Figure 3.8 describes the project.

Figure 3.7.
A TELEMENTORING SCIENCE PROJECT

I am looking for classroom teachers (with access to a network connection for their class) who are interested in participating in an electronically mediated science education project with me and my students in Geology 143 (The History of Life) this semester. Interested students in my geology class are receiving training in e-mail, newsgroups, and network (Internet) information search and retrieval. I want them to develop skill in electronic communication by linking electronically with elementary and middle school classroom teachers and students and serving as information brokers in support of instructional modules, in those classrooms, on the history of life (dinosaurs, mammal evolution, extinctions, etc.) and history of the earth (origin of the Appalachians, opening of the Atlantic, etc.), and the functioning of the earth (plate tectonics, etc.).

In order to accomplish this, we need participating classrooms with students and teachers interested in advancing their understanding of the earth by collaborating with me and my students. Because a very large number of my students (over 90) originally indicated their interest in participating, we need quite a few classrooms. I anticipate that teams of 3-5 students will work with each participating classroom, searching out answers to the classroom questions, either over the network, or through the library resources here on campus. That information would then be transmitted to the classroom, along with its source, including how to navigate to it, if it came from over the network.

"Ask-an-Expert" services have proliferated at astounding speeds. A comprehensive index to these resources is available on the Web (http://www.askanexpert.com/askanexpert/). In late 1997, this page linked users to more than 300 question-and-answer sites.

Question-and-answer activities also can be more long-lived and complex than simply sending a question to a Q-and-A service. Kay Corcoran, a middle school teacher in Mendocino, California, helped her students create questions for historians specializing in ancient history. Corcoran stated her educational goals in her project summary, which is excerpted in Figure 3.9.

Conversations with others online also can take on more fanciful characterizations, as in the case of impersonation activity structures.

Impersonations

Impersonation projects are those in which any (or all) of the participants communicate with one another "in character." At the University of Virginia, for example, history professor Jennings Waggoner "became" Thomas Jefferson via electronic mail for several local elementary classes studying Virginia history. His work is now carried on by a team of docents at Jefferson's home, Monticello, to benefit the larger number of K-12 students who use Virginia's Public Education Network

---

Figure 3.8.
ASK-A-GEOLOGIST SERVICE

Have you ever wondered about why California has so many earthquakes, and New York does not? Why is there so much oil in Texas, but not in Wisconsin? What are the deepest canyons in the United States? (The answer might surprise you!) While the answers to many of these questions might be as close as an encyclopedia, some questions are difficult to answer without checking many sources.

Beginning Monday, October 4, 1994, the USGS (U.S. Geological Service) will offer a new, experimental Internet service—Ask-A-Geologist. General questions on earth sciences may be sent by electronic mail to the Internet address: ask-a-geologist@octopus.wr.usgs.gov

All electronic mail to Ask-A-Geologist will be routed to the geologist of the day. The geologist will reply to your question within a day or two, or provide referrals to better sources of information. Please include an Internet-accessible return address in the body of your message.

(gopher://pen.k12.va.us:5000/11/Pav/Soc Studies/Jefferson/Letters).

Students who use the Elementary Book Conference on VaPEN (http://pen.k12.va.us/Anthology/Pav/) can communicate with characters from children's literature, such as Winnie the Pooh, Willie Wonka, and Ramona Quimby. These exchanges are coordinated and studied by Jeradi Hochella, of Appalachian State University, and Jan Stuhlmann, of Louisiana State University.

Following the popular example set by Kurt Grosshans' advanced placement chemistry students in Virginia with their Ask Mr. Science project, participants in the Math Forum (http://forum.swarthmore.edu/) at Swarthmore College offer the services of "Dr. Math" (http://forum.swarthmore.edu/dr.math/), as shown in Figure 3.10.

Clearly, this is a rich and motivating way for students to use telecomputing tools to help them to explore many curriculum-related topics.

Information Collection and Analysis

Can the Internet bring knowledge to the K-12 classroom? Interestingly, the answer is probably no. Surprised? You won't be, when you consider the differences between knowledge and information.

Clearly, an enormous amount and variety of information is available on the Internet. It comes in many different forms: text, pictures, video clips, sound files, and software. It comes via several different formats: Gopher, World Wide Web, electronic mail, conferencing, real-time interaction, and direct file transfer. But is this knowledge?

Many, like Taylor and Swartz (1991), would say no. To these scholars, knowledge is the

Figure 3.9.
A MULTIPLE PERSPECTIVES ACTIVITY

To enliven and engage the middle school learner, project-based units based on guided research are a popular feature in the History/Social Science curriculum. Typical research projects utilize the resources of school and community libraries, and students need to learn to read information closely and thoughtfully. With the availability of telecommunication resources for research on chosen topics, they soon discover that "historical fact" is open to interpretation, contradiction, and occasional controversy.

As a culmination activity to their research project presentations, those students who have been "critical readers," who have recorded inconsistencies, who have exhausted their resources, and have unanswered questions may utilize listservs to provide clarification.

A variety of history listservs abound, and the discussions cover a wide range of topics. Not only will 6th and 7th graders see that ancient history is alive and well, but that "historical fact" is open to interpretation based on evidence. History listservs provide an excellent opportunity for middle school students to observe the give and take of inquiry and to dialogue with the experts.

result of the process of knowing, which can only occur when learners actively construct what they know, using information in this process.

Larsen declares that the confusion between knowledge and information "is perhaps one of the most serious and widespread mistakes in the current use of information technology, and it leads to the attitude that giving students information is identical to giving them knowledge" (quoted in Fox 1991, p. 224). He says that knowledge results when an individual personally transforms information. Knowledge is private; information is public. Knowledge, therefore, cannot be communicated; only information can be shared. Whenever an attempt to communicate knowledge is made, it is expressed as information, which other learn-

ers can choose to absorb and transform into knowledge, if they so desire.

This distinction, although it may strike you as purely semantic at first, is important to consider when deciding how to structure educational telecomputing activities. Some of the most motivating and successful activity structures are those that encourage students to collect and share information and then, most important, to use it to actively create higher-order ideas.

This section details five different types of information collection. Please note that the most common form of data collection on the Internet—using Web-based search engines to find information about a particular topic—is not an activity structure in and of itself. But it often is incorporated into any of the activity structures offered in this chapter. (Chapter 4 describes more of this process of teleresearch.)

**Figure 3.10.
ASK DR. MATH**

You can submit your K-12 math question using the above link or by sending e-mail to dr.math@forum.swarthmore.edu. Tell us what you know about your problem, and where you're stuck and we might be able to help you. Dr. Math will reply to you via e-mail, so please be sure to send us the right address. K-12 questions usually include what people learn in the U.S. from the time they're five years old through when they're about eighteen.

Information Exchange

There are many examples of thematically related information exchanges that have served as popular telecomputing activities. Students and their teachers from around the globe have collected, shared, and discussed:

- Student-written book reviews
- Summer and winter solstice information
- Children's voices (as sound files)
- Teenagers' fashion preferences
- Favorite quotes
- International eating habits
- Local weather conditions
- Children's hour-by-hour schedules of activities on a common day
- Recipes
- Observations about wild birds
- Family life customs and perspectives
- Insect identifications
- Immigration and emigration experiences
- International holiday customs
- Local and regional festivals
- Internet signature files
- Video letters
- Schoolground ecosystems
- School safety rules

This type of activity can involve many classes without becoming an overwhelming management task for teachers, and it is a particularly powerful application of telecomputing tools because students become both the creators and consumers of the information that they share.

Projects like these typically begin with a call for participation that is posted by a classroom teacher. Figure 3.11 shows such a message offered by Patti Weeg, coordinator of many KIDLINK projects.

Sometimes students initiate information collection projects, too. Figure 3.12 shows, in part, how two young men from two different countries advertised an international project about flags.

Sharing information that is intrinsically interesting to children on an international scale is an excellent way to engage them in authentic cultural exchange.

Database Creation

Some projects involve not only amassing but also organizing information into databases that participants and others can use for study. Successful information exchange activities can grow into database creation activities.

Students in Julie McMahan's 9th grade

computer literacy classes near Houston, Texas, for example, created a database of important world events by compiling and reflecting upon answers to the survey in Figure 3.13.

As telecomputing tools become more widely used in K-12 classrooms, student databases can be shared freely with the rest of the Internet community. Databases also can be created for students to access, using information that they supply. Venanzio Jelenic, for example, proposed the "Jaunts" project, in which students from many different countries collected pictures of their hometown signs (i.e., "Welcome to Port Sydney, home to 500 nice people and one old grouch"). Students sent these pictures along with text describing the town and themselves to Venanzio, who added the information to a growing Web page.

Figure 3.11.
AN INFORMATION EXCHANGE ABOUT PLACE NAMES
****
Loving Names
****

The Salisbury KIDCLUB kids searched for names of places that capture the "Valentine" spirit. Please add any other names of cities, towns, mountains, etc. We know there must be similar names in other countries but we just can't recognize them. You'll translate them for us? Many thanks!

Here's their list:

Darling Range Mts., Australia
Darlington, England
Darlington, South Carolina
Friend, Nebraska
Friendship, New York
Heart's Content, Newfoundland
Heart's Delight, Newfoundland
Honey Brooke, Pennsylvania
Honeygrove, Texas
Kissimmee, Florida
Love, Oklahoma
Lovejoy, Illinois
Loveland, Colorado
Loveland, Ohio
Lovelock, Nevada
Lovely, Kentucky
Loving, Texas
Lovington, Illinois
Valentine, Nebraska

—Kristi, Kelli, Hickory, Maggie, Mickey, Karen, and Nada

Figure 3.12.
AN INFORMATION EXCHANGE ABOUT FLAGS

KIDPROJ FLAGS PROJECT
Dear Friends,

We (Andraz and I) would like to organize a project. A project about flags. We are asking "kids" to send us a "drawing" of their flag and also a description. What do the colors mean, and maybe some history.

Please DRAW your flag, because "scanned" pictures are very big, and when we get a lot . . . then the hard drive will get too full. :)

—Andraz & Robbert

Figure 3.13.
WORLD EVENTS SURVEY

1. How old are you?
2. Are you a male or a female?
3. Where do you live? (City, State, Country)
4. What is the name of your school?
5. What was the most important event that happened in your school during the past year? (Please explain briefly why you feel this event was so important.)
6. What was the most important event that happened in your city or state during the past year? (Please explain briefly why you feel this event was so important.)
7. What was the most important event that happened in your country during the past year? (Please explain briefly why you feel this event was so important.)

Electronic Publishing

Another type of information collection and analysis occurs with the electronic publishing of a newspaper, literary magazine, or electronic journal. For example, students who worked with Priscilla Franklin of the Woolslair Elementary Gifted Center in Pittsburgh, Pennsylvania, created an "ethnic cookbook" with recipes supplied by students from all over the world. John Swang, director of the National Student Research Center (http://members.aol.com/nsrcmms/NSRC.html) at Mandeville Middle School in Louisiana, helps students to edit and publish both printed and electronic journals that feature the results of exemplary student research. And Gary Ritzenthaler coordinated the Global Student

News project (http://www.jou.ufl.edu/forums/gsn/), which made news stories and photographs created by high school students available via the Internet to student journalists all over the world.

Telefieldtrips

Organizers for the Global SchoolNet Foundation (http://www.gsn.org/index.html) encourage Internet-connected teachers and students to share observations and experiences made during local fieldtrips with teachers and students from other cities, states, and countries. One unusual example of such an electronic fieldtrip occurred when Jane Goodall took 60 children to visit the exotic animals on the Michael Jackson Ranch, teaching about their care and feeding, and sharing information about the issues associated with animal welfare. The students who visited the California ranch took other children's questions along with them so that they could find answers and report them back to the remotely located questioners. After the trip, the students shared both the answers that they discovered and their general observations and impressions of the experience.

Expeditions taken by subject-matter specialists also are shared on the Internet. In 1995, a team of archaeologists and bicyclists began an expedition to Central America, studying the ancient Mayan civilization as part of the MayaQuest project. This rich interdisciplinary project was first described, in part, as shown in Figure 3.14.

Figure 3.14.
A TELEFIELDTRIP TO STUDY THE MAYAN CIVILIZATION

During this school year, a kid-directed team of archaeologists and bicyclists will be using the latest technology to help illuminate one of the greatest mysteries of all time: the collapse of the ancient Maya Civilization.

Between February and May 1995, the team will travel through Guatemala, Belize, Honduras, and southern Mexico. On mountain bikes they'll carry Hi-8 cameras, laptop computers, and EXEC*SAT satellite transponders which will connect the team to an online audience featured on Prodigy and the Internet.

Students will be able to help direct the expedition and help answer questions by archaeologists in the field. CNN Newsroom will air weekly reports on the expedition's progress and students in Minnesota will produce live satellite programs with accompanying support curriculum available via the Internet. All Internet materials are available via Gopher, World Wide Web, or e-mail.

Figure 3.15.
A NASA-SPONSORED TELEFIELDTRIP

FOSTER On-line will plug an airborne astronomy missions group into cyberspace. These researchers fly on NASA's Kuiper Airborne Observatory with an infrared telescope at 41,000 feet; the altitude diminishes problems with atmospheric absorption. The women and men involved in this research will be based in both Hawaii and California in May and early June. During this time they hope to share the excitement of a NASA research project with K-12 classrooms via the Internet.

Frequent project updates will be sent almost every day. Students and teachers will be encouraged to send questions to the team via e-mail. Various background materials including articles, lesson plans, and images will be made available via gopher and FTP. A video documentary about the research team will be aired via satellite once per week. The remainder of this message will provide details on the various components.

This virtual expedition was so successful that MayaQuest is now a yearly event, and it offers rich and varied multidisciplinary, multi-level resources and activities. A visit to their beautiful Web site (http://www.mecc.com/internet/maya/maya.html) is strongly suggested.

NASA sponsored another exciting "vicarious expedition" that focused upon astronomical research and was dubbed FOSTER On-line. Figure 3.15 shows how it was announced.

Lessons learned during the FOSTER On-line project are available (http://info.isoc.org/HMP/PAPER/246/html/section4.html), as are details about other exciting NASA-sponsored telefieldtrips and educational resources (http://quest.arc.nasa.gov/OER/). Especially noteworthy is Passport to Knowledge's (http://quest.arc.nasa.gov/antarctica/passport.html) Live From Mars project (http://quest.arc.nasa.gov/mars/), which is described by its creators in Figure 3.16.

Figure 3.16.
GO TO MARS WITH NASA

In 1996 NASA launched two missions to Mars. The Mars Global Surveyor spacecraft took off in November and will arrive about nine months later to begin an orbital mission that will provide detailed mapping and weather information. The Mars Pathfinder spacecraft blasted away in December and will land on the Red Planet on July 4, 1997. Once landed, the mission plan calls for a micro-rover named Sojourner to begin wandering the Martian terrain, returning a wealth of new science data.

By participating in the Live from Mars project, you and your students can travel along! The project is targeted at the middle school grade levels, but will have appeal above and below that range.

Online expeditions can even help us to track animals' movements. The "Wolf Studies Project," organized by members of InforMNs (http://www.informns.k12.mn.us/), an educational Internet provider in Minnesota, in their words, "allowed students and teachers around the world to hear, see, and track radio-collared wolves in the Superior National Forest via the Internet."

Pooled Data Analysis

Information collections are particularly effective when data are gathered at multiple sites and then combined for numeric and/or pattern analysis. In the simplest of these activities, students electronically issue a survey, collect the responses, pool and analyze the results, and report their findings to all participants. One such project involved a group of students in St. Claire Shores, Michigan, who polled other students about the time that they spent watching television. Another group of students working through the National Student Research Center distributed a "quiz" to test respondents' knowledge about breast cancer. Tenth grade students studying civil justice in Monroe, Michigan, collected and analyzed responses to a survey of opinions on physician-assisted suicide.

These kinds of activities also have included projects in which students collect data at numerous and varied sites, then pool and analyze the information to reveal patterns about environmental problems. For example, Marita Moll's 6th year students in Ottawa, Ontario, coordinated an international study of ultraviolet radiation levels. Michele Wendel's students in Concord, New Hampshire, led an international monitoring project on low-level ozone readings. Figures 3.17 shows how Jim Meinke's students in Lakewood, California, proposed helping students at other locations create isogonic maps of the Earth's magnetic fields with this simple call for participation in a sophisticated project.

Clearly, pooled data activities hold much promise for involving students in large-scale research efforts that use mathematics and scientific methods to answer complex and interesting questions.

Figure 3.17.
INTERESTED IN A NEW WORLDWIDE EXPERIMENT? MAPPING THE EARTH'S MAGNETIC FIELD (ISOGONIC)

This experiment can involve many classrooms around the globe in

- Communications
- Measurement
- Mapping skills
- Calculation

It would involve a minimum of equipment at each school (or home) to conduct the experiment.

- World map
- Compass(es)
- Night observation of Polaris (North Star), Southern Cross for our southern neighbors

The experiment would involve many schools or homes involved in gathering the data from their latitude and longitude. How far off is your magnetic data from true north or south in your location? This data would be transmitted to us here at Lakewood High School, and we would send out a summary so that you could construct a worldwide magnetic map in your classroom. This would also lead to discussions on the locations of the magnetic poles as well as how to draw *iso* (or equal) lines. It might also lead to discussions of night sky movements around the constellations or how the magnetic field is thought to be created.

ARE YOU INTERESTED?

If you are interested in trying such an experiment, drop me a quick note at the address below.

—Jim Meinke, Lakewood High School

Problem Solving

Roger Lewin once said, "Too often we give children answers to remember rather than problems to solve" (Lincoln and Suid 1986, p. 100). Problem solving is one of the most beneficial educational opportunities that we can offer students of any age, and the Internet can be used to extend cooperative problem solving around the world. Educational problem-solving projects are, as yet, the least common kind of Internet activity with K-12 students, but they are among the best examples of how asynchronous connectivity can be used to support and enrich the curriculum. Seven different structures can be considered as part of the problem-solving genre.

Information Searches

With this type of online activity, students are provided with clues and must use reference sources (either electronic or paper-based) to solve problems. For example, Figure 3.18 shows how students with learning disabilities at Desert View High School challenged other students (with the assistance of their teacher, Michael McVey).

Figure 3.18.
PROBLEM SOLVING THROUGH AN INFORMATION SEARCH

Subject: A Challenge to All Students: Where Are We?

Dear Students,
My students are ready to challenge you. We have 40 postcards to give away (that's all we can afford right now) to students who are up to our challenge. We will send you a postcard from our city if you can guess who we are AND send us a set of clues about your own home. We want you to challenge us, too! Here are the clues. You can try to figure out the answers in teams and make a game of it or work as a group. Good luck. :-)

1. We can see Mexico on a clear day.
2. We rarely get snow.
3. Our city nickname is The Old Pueblo.
4. United States Supreme Court Justice O'Connor comes from our state.
5. Our state's birthday is on Valentine's Day.
6. We live south of the bird that rose from the ashes.
7. Mount Lemmon is in our backyard.
8. Our area code is (200 * 3) + 2
9. We have 300 days of sunshine a year.
10. We are the southernmost ski area in the United States.

McVey added a note for interested teachers, suggesting that their students use encyclopedias, atlases, and library resources to answer the questions.

Information search activities also can be of longer duration, and they can embody extensive and sophisticated research, analysis, and communication activities for participating students. A good example is the What's in a Name? project (http://www.edc.org/FSC/NCIP/TC_KIDLINk-kidproj.html#anchor 401970), which took place via KIDLINK interpersonal and informational communications facilities (i.e., the KIDLINK and KIDPROJ discussion lists, the KIDLINK Internet Relay Chat, and the KIDLINK Gopher, which can be reached through http://www.kidlink.org/). With this project, students were challenged to research sets of related names of people, examine name collections in the context of certain characteristics (such as mythological connections or cultural differences in naming practices), and then take the results of this research and analysis and share it electronically through written reports. Din Ghani, the organizer of this project from Newcastle upon Tyne in the United Kingdom, provided a detailed and richly conceived structure for the yearlong exploration, which organized students' work into multiple and multisite research, analysis, management, and work packages.

Peer Feedback Activities

Students in Trevor Owen's high school English classes in Toronto regularly posted the poems that they wrote to newsgroups sponsored by Simon Fraser University so that other students in Canada could offer feedback in an electronic version of process writing sessions. Owen also has been able to enlist the assistance of professional writers, such as poet Lionel Kearns, to offer constructive criticism—and to sometimes receive some of the same from students in response to pieces in progress. This Writers in Electronic Residence (http://www.edu.yorku.ca/wierhome/) project is now supported by a number of Canadian organizations, including York University. It helps students to explore many different types of writing.

Electronically assisted process writing also can take on other forms. For example, 14- and 15-year-olds from a number of different school sites participated in the Doomed Train project, organized and facilitated by Francis Achiu of Moanalua High School in Honolulu, Hawaii. This project concentrated upon the situation in Bosnia-Herzegovina by asking students to complete the activities described in Figure 3.19.

Note that this peer feedback activity asked students to concentrate their feedback primarily upon the *content* of one another's writing, while projects such as Writers in Electronic Residence ask students to concentrate primarily upon the *forms* through which content is communicated. In both cases, rich, geographically unlimited, constructively critical exchanges occur.

Parallel Problem Solving

With this activity structure, a similar problem is presented to students in several locations, which they solve separately at each site.

Then they share, compare, and contrast their varied problem-solving methods electronically. For example, middle school students on the statewide educational telecommunications network in Virginia (VaPEN) participated in an interdisciplinary project called Puzzle Now!, organized by Heidi Bernard. In this project, students from 25 sites within the state solved a common puzzle each week for eight weeks, comparing not only solutions but, more important, multiple methods for working the problem.

Figure 3.19.
A PEER FEEDBACK ACTIVITY ON BOSNIA-HERZEGOVINA

We plan to ask our students to write a persuasive essay that addresses the question: Should Bosnia-Herzegovina remain a confederation or be divided into Croat, Muslim, and Serb sections? The English classes will be divided up into six or seven teams consisting of four heterogeneously grouped students. Each team will be asked to select an ethnic group, take a side on this question, and present their arguments. Thus, we will have one Croat group arguing for confederation and another Croat group arguing for separation. The same will go for the other two ethnic groups so that each team will be different. We plan to put this lesson and question on the Internet and call for participation. The classes from around the world can select any of our teams to challenge. Through e-mail the students can exchange papers and offer rebuttals.

In another parallel problem-solving activity, elementary level students in different classrooms designed floating boats made out of 15-centimeter squares of aluminum foil to hold as many pennies as possible. Then they shared designs, problem-solving procedures, and experiences via electronic mail. This simple but powerful activity was coordinated by Barbara Leonard, a substitute teacher in central Michigan.

In conjunction with an Earth Day observance, students in many different grades and schools were challenged by David Warlick of Raleigh, North Carolina, to become "eco-entrepreneurs" by developing, in David's words, "an imaginative new product that could make a profit, but not impact on the environment." The product designs had to use at least 50 percent recycled materials. Students wrote and submitted sales pitches for their products on Earth Day, which Warlick compiled into a catalog. Student groups then used the electronic catalog to select and place fictitious orders for products. The sales statistics were then sent to all groups for review and discussion. This project has continued and expanded into the Eco-Marketing Project (http://www. landmark-project.com/eco-market/).

Sequential Creations

An intriguing kind of artistic problem solving has emerged on the Internet. Participants progressively and collaboratively create a written text, visual image, or computer program. For example, Yvonne Andres and Mary Jacks from Oceanside High School in California helped their students start a sequential text by encouraging them to write the first few stanzas of a poem about world peace. They then sent their work to students in a different school, who read the stanzas and added their own. This process continued until the poem had circled the world several times and had grown, understandably, to epic length.

Paul Fretheim organized students from all over North America to create a "Native American ChainStack." Students at participating sites created HyperStudio stacks on the Native American tribes found in their geographic locations. (HyperStudio is a hypertextual authoring tool in use in many schools.) They then combined these stacks into one large stack, creating a valuable and interactively accessible information resource.

John Ost organized students who participated in a monthly realtime "Writers' Corner" via the KIDLINK Internet Relay Chat channel to create short stories online, following plans like the ones in Figure 3.20.

Telepresent Problem Solving

Telepresent problem-solving sessions bring together participants from different geographic locations and time zones in realtime to either participate in a computer-mediated meeting or, without direct electronic contact, do similar activities at different project sites. For example, students using the KIDCLUB Internet Relay Chat can participate on most Saturdays in discussions organized by Patti Weeg, a Title I teacher in Salisbury, Maryland. On one Saturday, students chatted about what they would do "if they were in charge of the school." Weeg suggested that they think about

Figure 3.20.
ONLINE STORIES THAT GROW IN THE TELLING

Let's build a short story as a group online. Don't worry about punctuation or anything other than building a story. So come to the meeting with three nouns, verbs, and adjectives that you'd like to see as part of the story.

For example:
- Nouns: cat, ball, string
- Verbs: hit, swat, swallow
- Adjectives: big, hard, green

If I told the story myself, I might write the following:

I have a big cat named Maryann. Actually, Maryann was a boy cat but I didn't know it so I named him Maryann. One day he saw a green, hard ball lying in a corner. He dashed over to the ball and swatted it with his paw. The ball shot across the room and suddenly flew back and hit Maryann right in the nose. "What happened?" he purred to himself. Maryann carefully nuzzled the ball forward with his nose. To his surprise, he saw a long gray piece of string attached to the ball. . . .

Well, you get the idea. Now, when everyone else comes prepared with words, that story won't just have my nouns and verbs *or my original story idea.* Instead, it will be a composite story that grows as each of us adds our choice of words and ideas to each sentence.

Each one of us will take turns being the narrator and building the sentence from the words made available by the group. (Lord knows how this will work if lots of people come to the meeting. But we'll make it work.)

We can put whatever rules we want on the story telling. But we'll have to decide those rules when we meet. And those rules can always change—just like they will as you learn to write your own stories and develop your own style of writing.

answers to questions such as those in Figure 3.21 to help them prepare for the virtual gathering.

In a poignant virtual gathering involving all 67 school districts in Florida, students and teachers observed A Day Without Art on the 8th annual World AIDS Day. Sandy McCourtney and Sally Lucke, coordinators for the activities, describe the virtual gathering in Figure 3.22.

Telepresent problem-solving activities can incorporate use of multimedia, especially now that inexpensive interactive video-conferencing facilities are available on the Internet. For example, students from many different Internet sites helped to build CitySpace, a model of a virtual city hosted by the San Francisco Exploratorium (http://www.exploratorium.edu/). Students had previously sent in stories, scanned photographs, hand-drawn pictures, audio samples, 3-D models,

40

and other creations about the neighborhoods and "imaginary spaces" in which they lived. These were then used by teams of students, artists, and developers to create CitySpace, which could be explored using online multimedia tools, such as Cornell University's popular CU-SeeMe freeware (http://www.indstate.edu/msattler/sci-tech/comp/CU-SeeMe/index.html).

Figure 3.21.
A TELEPRESENT PROBLEM-SOLVING ACTIVITY

1. If I were principal, what would I change about our school? Why?
2. What would I keep the same? Why?
3. As a student, do you feel that your views are respected?
4. Do you have any part in decision making in any of your classes?

Simulations

Online simulations require the most coordination and maintenance of all activity structures. But the depth of learning they offer and the task engagement participants display often convince project organizers to spend the additional time and effort necessary to make them work. Notable examples of successful online simulations include Academy One's NESPUT (National Educational Simulations Project Using Telecommunications) activities, coordinated by Bob Morgan. These collaborative projects simulated space shuttle launches, histori-

cal space missions, space colony design, ozone layer repair, and stock market investments, to name just a few. Activities of this type depend upon person-to-person communication to create the simulated situation.

Simulations also can be organized around the use of software that creates virtual worlds for students to explore. The National Center for Supercomputing Applications (NCSA), for

---

Figure 3.22.
OBSERVING WORLD AIDS DAY

THE ACTIVITIES: Schools representing all 67 Florida districts will submit visual and discourse statements in the form of a blindfold and awareness statement. These blindfolds will be draped on the statuary located in the Ringling Museum Courtyard, signifying the message that at times, regarding AIDS, "we are unaware and cannot see." In a symbolic gesture, the blindfolds on the museum statuary will be removed, once the on-site and electronic dialogs have commenced.

THE INVITATION is this:
1. Send an electronic awareness message, a message of support, or a "factoid" (fact) related to AIDS and/or
2. Design a piece of cyberspace-cloth to blindfold one of the statues!

Please limit messages to no more than one screen; if you intend to send a graphic file, please send an e-mail (text) message to the address below to specify the paint and compression program you will be using.

example, permitted students to use supercomputing facilities at the Lawrence Livermore Laboratory remotely to help them to solve proposed projects in science and mathematics. Sophisticated simulation software—which allowed students to explore subjects such as climate modeling, ray tracing, molecular configuration, or plant growth modeling—was made available by NCSA to students and teachers at their school sites, along with teacher education materials and curricular integration models. A similar collection of simulation projects called BRIDGE (http://www.ncsa.uiuc.edu/Edu/Simulations/) is now available from NCSA's Education Group.

Social Action Projects

It should be no surprise to global citizens living near the beginning of the 21st century that the Internet can serve as a context for "humanitarian, multicultural, action-oriented telecommunications projects" (Ed Gragert, I*EARN: http://www.iearn.org/iearn/) that involve the future leaders of our planet: our children.

Mike Burleigh, for example, organized students worldwide using KIDLINK Internet Relay Chats to participate with his students at the Cedars Primary School in London (http://metrotel.co.uk/cedars/cedars.html) in a 24-hour telecommunications vigil that helped to raise money for children in Lebanon. Figure 3.23 shows, in part, how he described the activity to potential participants.

Nina Hansen, from the Timothy Edwards Middle School in South Windsor, Connecticut, organizes students from all over the world

---

Figure 3.23.
RAISING MONEY FOR CHILDREN IN LEBANON

Dear KIDLINK Friends,

We are one of the KIDCLUBs on KID-PROJ trying to find things which we can do to prove the KIDLINK fourth question that we are "thinking globally and acting locally to make the world a better place."

We have decided to have a sponsored IRC [Internet Relay Chat] link to raise money which we will send to the support UNICEF projects in Lebanon.

There will be six of us and we will be staging a 24-hour telecommunications vigil at the Cedar School, London, UK.

We will be meeting after school on Friday, 11th February, and will hope to receive messages of support from KIDLINK people around the world.

This will be reported in the local press. Some of us will be sleeping (the tough ones will stay awake).

---

each year to Save the Beaches (http://ednhp.hartford.edu/WWW/Nina/Beaches2.html) by planning and participating in beach sweeps. In Figure 3.24, she describes part of the organization of the project in 1995.

After reading U.S. Vice President Al Gore's *Earth in the Balance*, students from classrooms in California, Tennessee, Virginia, and London collaborated to "investigate the problems created by water run-off and to design a public awareness program that [could] be implemented in their own communities, and then shared and replicated globally" as part of the SAFER (Student Ambassadors for Environmental

41

Reform) Water Project. This work incorporated several Internet-based video teleconference meetings of the four research teams and their subject-matter guests. They then televised project results nationally during National Science and Technology week in 1994. The project was coordinated by Yvonne Andres and Al Rogers of the Global SchoolNet Foundation, with support from the National Science Foundation and many commercial networks and corporations.

It is interesting to note that many of the more sophisticated, interdisciplinary, and authentic online problem-solving projects focus participants' attention upon the problem to solve rather than the "answers to remember" or the telecommunication technologies used to share information. This clear emphasis upon the *process* of learning rather than the technologies that facilitate it or the answers to which the process leads is one of the characteristics that makes Internet-based interpersonal exchange, information collection and analysis, and problem solving so potentially powerful.

Figure 3.24.
SAVING THE BEACHES

The Save the Beaches Project is getting under way full force. In order to meet the May 30th deadline, schools are in the process of putting together a schedule and planning their beach sweeps. Each school is coordinating the project according to what works best for it. On Lake Erie, teachers were concerned over what types of litter students might encounter. To help alleviate any health hazards, experts from the State Health Department were called in to give students tips on what to do should they encounter any potentially dangerous litter. Here in Connecticut, all students will be supplied with rubber gloves and will be required to wear them during the clean-up. Precautions such as these will ensure both an educational and safe experience.

The most exciting aspect of the project is the wide range of locations that will be participating. At this writing there are at least 12 of the United States represented, two provinces in Canada, and the countries of Brazil, Costa Rica, Denmark, Portugal, Australia, and Japan have assured us they will be sending data.

Teachers as Facilitators of Teleresearch

The Internet now offers more than 18 million hosts, or computers, to which you can connect to access information. It has grown at a rate of 80 to 100 percent per year since 1989 (Quarterman 1997b). One estimate says that on average, a new Internet host is added about every 30 minutes (Calcari 1994). Obviously, teachers and students have access to abundant information, and the amount of that information is growing at a staggering speed.

Yet as mentioned in Chapter 3, merely accessing information should not be confused with constructing knowledge. The making of knowledge is an active, holistic, and idiosyncratic process for each learner, which can be greatly enhanced with a teacher's guidance. But how can teachers provide such direction when they themselves are relative newcomers to the overwhelming amount and variety of information available online?

Five Purposes for Searching

The usual answer to that question is technological—and insufficient. Information searching programs, such as veronica in Gopherspace, and search engines such as AltaVista on the World Wide Web, are powerful, useful tools that can help students locate large numbers of diverse and timely documents. In schools with the luxuries of easy access and flexible class schedules, students and teachers happily "surf the Internet," impressed with the range, amount, and appearance of all that can be unearthed about a particular area of inquiry. In a sense, they become Information Age hunters and gatherers in cyberspace, sharing news of the richest locations by exchanging addresses with members of their virtual clans. Yet it is here, at the point of information access, that many efforts to create knowledge falter. What should students *do* with information once they locate it? How can the fruits of the hunt be turned into food for the clan?

Part of the answer to this question lies in a plan for seeking information. If students know clearly how they will use the information that they locate, they increase their chances for purposeful searching rather than aimless surfing. Teachers can help students focus on specific purposes and formulate and carry out these plans. In fact, my virtual travels on the Internet have revealed five teacher-directed purposes for students' searching.

To Practice Information-Seeking Skills

Brian Callahan, a teacher working with public television station WHRO in Norfolk, Virginia, organized several grade-level divisions of The Great Computer Challenge Internet Scavenger Hunt to help his students collaboratively hone their information-seeking skills. Figure 4.1 contains some of the rules for this team-oriented competition. Figure 4.2 contains several of the questions provided to teams in grades 3–5.

As these rules and questions show, students were to practice, reflect upon, and share their Internet information-seeking strategies. (I also should mention, as did Callahan in his directions to students, that an additional requirement for the activity was to have fun!)

Honing information-seeking skills is an important prerequisite for much of what students do online related to their curricular studies. It should not be forgotten, though, that developing these skills is but a means to an end. The synthesis and evaluation of multiple types, formats, and sources of information are truly at the heart of knowledge construction. These are the focus of the four purposes that follow.

To Learn About a Topic or Answer a Question

Much online searching serves the purpose of learning about a topic or answering a question. For example, William Gathergood coordinated an activity called The Reynoldsburg Geography Project (http://archives.gsn.org/mar96/0014.html). The primary learning goals for this activity are listed in Figure 4.3.

Participants were paired with student partners from different countries, then asked to get to know their keypals through introductory

---

Figure 4.1.
RULES FOR THE GREAT COMPUTER CHALLENGE NETWORK

On your marks. . . .Welcome to the first ever Great Computer Challenge Internet Scavenger Hunt! There are three parts to the Scavenger Hunt: The Questions, The Log, and the Team Defense. Although this is a competition, we're much more interested in helping students learn about the Internet. Please keep teacher involvement to a minimum.

You will have a little over two weeks to answer the questions. Please pay close attention to the submission deadlines on page 2.

The Questions (please see attached page)
Each question has a different point value. Please try to answer every question, but remember: we're interested in not only the right answer, but how you get the answer.

The Log
Each team is required to keep a detailed Log telling us how you got your answers. There is no set format for the Log—just make sure it tells us everything. The more detailed the Log, the better. Even if you don't get the right answer, you'll probably get partial credit for trying.

The Team Defense
On the day of the competition, judges will ask each team a series of questions. Team members will be judged on the quality of their responses.

---

letters and 30 "icebreaker interview" questions. At this point, the project took on an interesting and powerful dimension, as Gathergood describes in Figure 4.4.

Please note that online information gathering often complements telecollaborative activity, as we see in this keypal project. In fact, we could argue that information seeking and synthesis as stand-alone activities have limited educational benefit for most students. Therefore, it is important to consider ways in which information can be collaboratively examined and critiqued.

To Review Multiple Perspectives on an Issue

Students often seem convinced that there are discrete and simply stated answers to many questions. Fortunately, the world is much more complex and interesting than that. Online information seeking can help students consider multiple perspectives about issues. For example, Kay Corcoran, a middle school teacher in Mendocino, California, helped her students formulate questions for historians who specialize in ancient history, as was mentioned in Chapter 3. This was a culminating activity, leading 6th and 7th grade students to "extend their research . . . on ancient history topics."

Figure 4.2.
SOME QUESTIONS FOR THE GREAT COMPUTER CHALLENGE NETWORK

2. What is the phone number for VA.PEN? (2 points)
3. What does VA.PEN stand for? (5 points)
7. What are the complete lyrics to "Won't You Be My Neighbor?" (7 points) [Hint: Mr. Rogers sings the song and makes his home on Learning Link.]
10. Who is Linda Berry? Send her an e-mail message. (10 points)

Bonus Question
13. What month and year, according to the NASA Fleet Manifest, is flight 63 scheduled for? (10 points)

The basis for this project is rich and educationally sound. Corcoran summarizes her project in Figure 4.5.

Alternative perspectives on an issue also can be gathered from files of information stored on Internet-accessible servers. For example, Din Ghani, the organizer for KIDLINK's "What's in a Name?" project (http://www.edc.org/FSC/NCIP/TC_KIDLINk-kidproj.html#anchor401970), first mentioned in Chapter 3, posted a list of helpful Internet-based genealogical resources to assist participants worldwide with their online and offline explorations of the etiologies, similarities, and differences among related groups of surnames and naming conventions in different parts of the world. Ghani, who moderated this telecollaborative project from Newcastle Upon Tyne in the United Kingdom, also provided a list of offline resources to help students locate information about the names or naming practices that they were researching. In this way, he illustrated an important and often overlooked aspect of the educational use of Internet resources. Information accessed online might be more recent, varied, and plentiful than what is available locally, but no matter how much it is hyped by technocentric advocates, one kind should not replace the other. Instead, all information should be used in combination and according to the requirements of each learning situation.

Figure 4.3.
LEARNING GOALS FOR THE REYNOLDSBURG GEOGRAPHY PROJECT

A. Hone students' skills in researching scientific and social information and map interpretation
B. Encourage students to communicate with others in other countries.
C. Help students to develop an understanding of the differences between scientific fact, presumption, and errors based on misinformation based upon stereotypes and prejudice.

To Solve an Authentic Problem

Advocates of constructivist learning and teaching emphasize the importance of students exploring and finding solutions to real-world, complex problems. Online information seeking can greatly assist these efforts. Martha McPherson's students in Fort Worth, Texas,

Figure 4.4.
LEARNING ABOUT LIFE IN OTHER COUNTRIES

After sending [letters] to their partners, the students will then be instructed to learn as much as possible about the other student's country through research. They may look at maps, books, magazines, and any computer-generated data they can find. After the research is complete, each student must write "A Day in the Life of the Other Student." The paper should include what each student thinks the other student's life is like. What are schools like? What do the students do for fun? What kind of work/responsibilities do they have outside of school? What is family life like? What are most students' attitudes about the future?

These questions should be answered to the best ability of the student who has researched the other country. So, if John Smith of central Ohio is working with a student in Japan, he would communicate with a student from there, and then begin research, using as many sources as are available to him. He will then write a paper entitled "A Day in the Life of _____." The student in Japan will do the same thing, studying the American student.

When the papers are finished, they are sent to the student in that country. When each student receives the paper about [his or her] life, the student will critique it. Obviously, students will discover mistakes. John Smith may not understand how Japanese life has become modernized while the Japanese student may have false assumptions about what Americans do with their leisure time.

In the critique, each student should point out which observations are correct and which are wrong. Then each will write about what his or her day-to-day life is really like. In this way, students will use research tools to learn about real people in other cultures, and have the opportunity to separate myth from fact—stereotypical prejudice from actual social behavior.

used information culled from Internet resources, data generated through student-written and administered surveys, and information available via electronic discussions with subject-matter experts to discover why the horned lizard is endangered. Her planning overview of the project posted to statewide newsgroups in Texas read as follows: "Students will use online research and survey instruments to collect data throughout the United States, Canada, Mexico, and Central America on the Horned Lizard. This information will be pooled and analyzed to discover reasons why this species is now endangered.

Electronic mentoring will be provided by scientists from Texas A&M."

Greg Rawls's junior high school students in Conroe, Texas, used online resources to both identify and explore local and larger scale social problems, as explained in Figure 4.6.

Gail Carmack's high school biology students used Internet resources via TENET, the Texas Education Network, to explore the scientific and social challenges presented by AIDS and other immuno-suppressive diseases through a well-constructed project entitled Students Exploring Cyberspace, or SECs. Figure 4.7 details their work.

Figure 4.5.
EXPERIENCING MULTIPLE PERSPECTIVES ON ANCIENT HISTORY

To enliven and engage the middle school learner, project-based units based on guided research are popular features in the History/Social Science curriculum. Typical research projects use the resources of school and community libraries, and students need to learn to read information closely and thoughtfully. With the availability of telecommunication resources for research on chosen topics, they soon discover that "historical fact" is open to interpretation, contradiction, and occasional controversy.

As a culmination activity to their research project presentations, those students who have been "critical readers," who have recorded inconsistencies, who have exhausted their resources, and have unanswered questions may use listservs to provide clarification.

A variety of history listservs abound, and the discussions cover a wide range of topics. Not only will 6th and 7th graders see that ancient history is alive and well, but that "historical fact" is open to interpretation based on evidence. History listervs provide an excellent opportunity for middle school students to observe the give and take of inquiry and to dialogue with the experts.

Note that the culminating activity for these students' exploration does not stop with their own edification. Instead, they share the fruits of their new understanding with others by producing instructional multimedia packages for younger students and using computer conferencing facilities to directly assist these students in their learning. This points to an important goal for use of information collected online: to publish syntheses and critical appraisals from a wide range of resources. In this way, the results of students' explorations can become information for other students to discover.

To Publish Information Overviews for Other Students to Use

Perhaps the single most important trend in the evolution of online resources is the development of a technologically simple way for Internet explorers to share the fruits of their labors worldwide. The most common way to do this is with a locally maintained but internationally accessible World Wide Web server. In early 1997, more than 7,000 K–12 schools in the world had such WWW servers (http://web66.coled.umn.edu/schools.html), and this number promises to grow rapidly by the turn of the century.

Several teleresearch projects incorporate publication efforts into the structure of students' activities. One example is the SECs project mentioned earlier. The Earth's Crust and Plate Tectonics Project (http://environment.negev.k12.il/platline.htm)—a multidisciplinary, interdisciplinary, and international effort organized by Hannah Sivan and David Lloyd from Sde Boker, Israel—requested that students create databases and WWW pages to summarize their discoveries of how phenomena relating

Figure 4.6.
SOLVING AUTHENTIC PROBLEMS

The "Problems" program is a student-based, problem-solving project in which students focus on the process involved in determining interdisciplinary, real-world solutions to local and societal issues. Students use online resources to research a topic, send out surveys to collect additional data, and exchange e-mail with experts and content specialists for guidance. It is expected that the project will be ongoing throughout the year with students producing a technical paper as a result of their research.

to plate tectonics appear in their daily lives. And in Project Population (http://www.tiac.net/users/mjharris/census2.html), organizer Martha J. Harris from Wayland, Massachusetts, requests that participants examine local historical census data to identify and eventually explain "[time] periods of rapid growth or decline." By publishing these local analyses on the Project Population Web Page, participants from all over the United States will soon be able to deduce common patterns (and perhaps causes) of population changes across sites.

There are numerous examples of synthesized information published online. One has to explore only a few of the many K–12 servers online to see evidence of this trend. Fortunately, Stephen Collins has made such exploration easy (http://web66.coled.umn.edu/schools.html). This Web page contains links to the great majority of K–12

servers plus sites set up by other organizations for the benefit of K–12 students and teachers. It is updated frequently and supports use of any WWW browser, including Lynx.

Figure 4.7.
LEARNING AND TEACHING ABOUT AIDS

Project SECs [Students Exploring Cyberspace] will allow biology and social studies students to study AIDS and other current topics in a multinational, interdisciplinary fashion. Students will use TENET resources such as Gopher, Veronica, Archie, Telnet, and FTP to research current information about AIDS pathology, epidemiology, treatment, and social implications. Additionally, they will communicate with students from other countries through e-mail to find out how AIDS impacts other societies. They will then produce multimedia packages that can be used to teach [about] AIDS at feeder junior high schools. High school students will use TENET newsgroups to mentor junior high students who are also studying AIDS.

Teleharvesting, Teleprocessing, and Beyond

Those of you raised in urban environments might be surprised to learn, as I was, that crop harvesting is not composed primarily of the collection and bundling of mature plants. Instead, it involves mostly the *processing* of gathered crops, getting them ready for sale or consumption. The same is true for teleharvest-

50

ed (Gunn 1995) information, which has been remotely cultivated, perhaps by groups of K–12 students and their teachers. The effective processing of Internet information—that is, its use by learners in the construction of knowledge—is a principal challenge to learners and teachers. We have much to learn and share about the art and practice of teleharvesting,

teleprocessing, and their natural successor: the sharing of constructed knowledge, which becomes information for other students through telepublished documents. Diana Paulina (1996), a teacher at the CEC Alternative School in Iowa City, Iowa, cleverly dubbed this important process *teleplanting*.

Eight Steps to Designing a Telecollaborative Project

Eventually (probably sooner, rather than later), your teacher-students will want to know how to put the curriculum-based educational telecomputing activities that they have designed into action. An important point to remember is that the logistics of directing a telecollaborative project are *not* intuitive. Because of the context in which communication takes place—often time-shifted and text-only—project collaborators must make many, often subtle, adjustments to ensure that both content and tone of their contributions are clear.

Many teachers prefer to first integrate telecomputing activities into their curriculum by joining a project that someone else has designed and organized. If this is the case with your teachers, the best place to find information about projects needing partners is the Global SchoolNet's international Projects Registry Page (http://www.gsn.org/pr/index.html), which lists both ongoing and one-time projects according to when they will accept new participants. However, if your teachers are ready to create and implement their own projects, the following guidelines will be helpful. They describe the design and implementation of a telecomputing activity through a series of eight steps.

Step 1: Choose Curriculum-Related Goals

At best, access to telecomputing facilities in most schools is limited. Therefore, when designing an online activity it is very important to be sure that learning goals

• Are tied directly to the curriculum and

• Could not be accomplished at all, or as well, using traditional teaching and learning tools.

By fulfilling these two criteria, teachers take the first step in ensuring maximum time-efficiency and cost-effectiveness of their telecomputing work.

When choosing curriculum-based goals for an online activity, teachers should consider what students will learn as they participate (the content goals), what they will do online, and whether that activity matches a process goal. Most e-mail projects, for example, require participants to write to an audience of peers. The teacher should question whether that authentic writing task is among his or her curriculum goals.

Step 2: Choose the Activity's Structure

There are a number of different ways to organize online projects. Chapter 3 describes these activity structures, which can be used at many grade levels and in any curriculum area.

They were conceptualized by reviewing hundreds of successful online projects that classroom teachers created, tested, and shared via the Internet.

Teachers just beginning to use the Internet often are unfamiliar with effective models for structuring online projects. The reason is because the attributes of the medium create a unique context for teaching and learning. For example, communication often is asynchronous. Communication also is widely distributed, text-only, and quickly turned around. That is why teachers should stop at this point in the planning process to review possible activity structures and choose or create the most appropriate ones.

To date, I have identified 18 activity structures, and new ones continually emerge as more teachers and students learn to use the Internet. Figure 5.1 reviews these structures and their three genres from Chapter 3.

Step 3: Explore Examples of Other Online Projects

Once teachers have chosen the activity's structure, it may be helpful to see how other teachers have organized and described similar projects. Reviewing one good example of a project can save 100 hours of planning time. Many project descriptions are freely available on the Internet. Sample projects indexed by activity structures are accessible on the University of Illinois Learning Resource Server (http://www.ed.uiuc.edu/Activity-Structures/). Notable collections of project ideas also can be found at these Web sites:

- Blue Web'n Applications Library: http://www.kn.pacbell.com/wired/bluewebn/
- British Council InterLink Projects: http://www.interlink.org.nz/projects/project1.html
- Electronic Elementary Magazine (E-LINK): http://www.inform.umd.edu/EdRes/Topic/Education/K-12/MDK12_Stuff/homepers/emag/
- EnviroNet's Environmental Awareness Projects:
  http://earth.simmons.edu/
- I*EARN's Social Action Projects: http://www.igc.apc.org/iearn/projects.html
- KIDLINK: http://www.kidlink.org/english/index.html
- NASA's Internet in the Classroom Projects: http://quest.arc.nasa.gov/interactive/
- NickNacks Telecollaborations: http://www1.minn.net:80/~schubert/EdHelpers.html
- SchoolNet Projects: http://www.stemnet.nf.ca/Projects/RINGS/current.html
- Telemation Project: http://www.telis.org/telis/telemat/telemat.htm
- The WebQuest Page: http://edweb.sdsu.edu/webquest/webquest.html
- oz-TeacherNet Curriculum Projects: http://owl.qut.edu.au/oz-teachernet/projects/projects.html

Step 4: Determine the Details

Participants associated with the Global SchoolNet Foundation, which originated in southern California as the FrEdMail network, have perhaps the most experience helping teachers to design, organize, and carry out collaborative telecomputing projects. They shared some of their best advice in a helpful article published several years ago (Rogers, Andres, Jacks, and Clausen 1990, also available at http://www.ed.uiuc.edu/guidelines/RAJC.html).

Figure 5.1
18 ACTIVITY STRUCTURES

Interpersonal Exchange
- Keypals
- Global Classrooms
- Electronic Appearances
- Telementoring
- Question-and-Answer Activities
- Impersonations

Information Collection and Analysis
- Information Exchange
- Database Creation
- Electronic Publishing
- Telefieldtrips
- Pooled Data Analysis

Problem Solving
- Information Searches
- Peer Feedback Activities
- Parallel Problem Solving
- Sequential Creations
- Telepresent Problem Solving
- Simulations
- Social Action Projects

In that article, they made it very clear that a detailed project description is essential for success. They suggested that the following elements be included in every description of and plan for a telecomputing project:

54

- The project's **title**.
- The project's educational **purpose(s)**.
- A name and an e-mail address for the project **organizer or contact person**.
- The **curricular areas** that the project addresses.
- The approximate **grade levels** for which the project is designed.
- The **number of collaborators** who will be accepted.
- A **summary** of the project's plan.
- Directions for **registration**, or joining the project.
- A detailed **timeline** for the project, including specific **tasks** to be completed and all **interim deadlines**.
- Specific, ordered **procedures for participation** in the project.
- A sample of **student work** that the project will generate.
- How the project will **end**, including plans for how project results will be shared with all participants.

Waugh, Levin, and Smith (1994, also available at http://www.ed.uiuc.edu/guidelines/WLS.html) suggest that teachers should not specify grade levels or age groups during initial project planning because cross-age communication can be beneficial to students. They also recommend that timelines be kept somewhat flexible to accommodate inevitable scheduling conflicts or technical failures. Finally, they suggest planning in a way that distributes project ownership, focusing upon specific, rather than general, topics for study.

Margaret Riel, facilitator for the many successful "Learning Circle" projects (http://www.iearn.org/iearn/circles/lc-home.html) and Passport to Knowledge (http://quest.arc.nasa.gov/antarctica/passport.html) virtual expeditions, recommends that teachers plan to network with more than one or two other classrooms. Ideally, 5 to 10 classes should collaborate on an extended project. In this way, it is easier to take advantage of the cultural and regional diversity of participants. And even if several classes encounter technical difficulties, fruitful communication can continue (Riel 1992).

Riel also points out that it is important to make sure that the amount and scope of information requested from participating classes is reasonable. She suggests planning projects so that they fit into the larger framework of classroom activity. In addition, the information created through telecollaboration should be of interest to a wide local audience of students, teachers, parents, and other community members. When the project is complete, the fruits of the students' and teachers' labors can be proudly shared, and teachers can garner or strengthen community support for educational networking.

Once these details are decided upon, teachers need to create a detailed file with project specifics and upload it to their Internet account. They will include this information in e-mail notes to those who contact them about joining their project. Inviting others to join in their project is the next part of this process.

Step 5: Invite Telecollaborators

Once you have decided upon all the details of your project, it is time to write a brief description of the project to post in public online areas that are frequented by other K–12 teachers with Internet access. Waugh and colleagues (1994) suggest that this brief file be used to advertise the availability of the project, and teachers should offer to send more details to interested parties through private e-mail. My experience organizing online projects has confirmed the effectiveness of this method, especially because the Internet addresses of interested teachers can be used to create an e-mail distribution list to be applied when organizing other projects in which these teachers might be interested.

New projects can be registered either at the Global SchoolNet Projects Registry Web page (http://www.gsn.org/pr/index.html) or by electronic mail (proj.register@gsn.org). Figure 5.2 shows the information posted for potential collaborators to review.

Rogers and others (1990) suggest that teachers try out a project idea with a small group of close colleagues before opening it up to the larger online community. In this way, complications with the plan can be addressed on a small scale with relatively little embarrassment.

Step 6: Form the Telecollaborative Group

As soon as they receive a response, teachers should send a reply message to each inter-

ested participant. Often, this message will initiate teachers-to-organizer planning discussions online. The message should contain the file that they prepared in advance, which lists all project details. This file should specify procedures for registering, the maximum number of classes that can take part, and the deadline for registering.

Figure 5.2
REGISTERING NEW PROJECTS

- Name of the Project
- First and Last Name of the Contact Person
- E-mail Address of the Contact Person
- Brief Description of the Project
- Recommended for Students of Ages (e.g., 10–13)
- When Does the Project Begin?
- How Long (approximately) Will the Project Last?
- Educational/Learning Objectives of the Project
- (Optional) The URL Where Potential Participants Can Find Additional Information
- How Will You Share the Results of Your Project?

Citation: http://www.gsn.org/pr/addproj.html

Project organizers can then save the information from each teacher's registration message in a file in their Internet account, which they will download later to use while coordinating the project. The registration should include the teacher's name, full Internet address, school name, school location, school telephone number (to use only in "emergencies"), the number of students who will participate, and their grade levels or age groups.

Teachers should respond to each request for registration as quickly as possible, perhaps using another prepared file that contains the additional information about how to begin work on the project. Waugh and colleagues (1994) suggest that this initial contact can be used to distribute project ownership by encouraging new participants to collaborate on the finer details of the project.

If more teachers want to register for the project than the organizer can handle or if the organizer wants to select participants based upon predetermined criteria, they should receive a friendly apology explaining why they cannot participate. If they agree, their Internet addresses could be retained as part of a distribution list to notify potential participants about future online projects.

Step 7: Communicate!

Online exchange is different from most other forms of communication in significant ways. It is asynchronous, primarily text-based, widely distributed across space and time, and relatively fast (that is, when the server isn't down). It also lacks the auditory and visual cues that we depend upon in face-to-face communication. Often, telecollaborators know very little about the contexts in which the others work, or how important project participation

is to each teacher or student. Delayed responses can be caused by a host of situations, from unannounced assemblies to student resistance to project work. Therefore, online talk requires somewhat different communications techniques if it is to be used for maximal educational benefit by students and teachers.

Because each activity structure requires a slightly different type and sequence of online interaction, I'll share only general suggestions for facilitating online discussion here. Educators undoubtedly will discover and share more as they communicate with other teachers and students online.

Waugh and others (1994) suggest that teachers

• Create a distribution list of all project participants so that periodic reports of progress and materials sent to meet interim deadlines are easily shared and filed.

• Sign all e-mail with all of the names of the people contributing to the message. I would add that including the school name and location is helpful, too.

• Provide a brief synopsis of the discussion to date before adding another perspective to the conversation. This provision will help all readers clearly understand the context in which the message's author is asking a question or making a comment.

• Be willing to share what you know (especially in terms of technical assistance) freely with newcomers, who can often feel intimidated when first online.

• Focus discussions carefully and solely upon the preselected topics for collaborative study.

• Use short, private messages to keep communications alive. For example, Waugh and colleagues (1994) suggest "return receipt messages" can be sent to team members if the recipient is busy. This tells them that their message has been received and will be answered soon. "Cheerleader messages" recognize and praise exceptional efforts. "Ping messages" privately ask telecollaborators who have not posted something recently whether they are still participating in the project. "Thank-you messages" express appreciation and encourage participation. "Reminder messages" are an important addition to this list. They prompt participants about approaching deadlines, and they can help assure a project's success within typically constrained school schedules.

Rogers and colleagues (1990) suggest that teachers involve students in ongoing facilitation of their projects whenever possible. I would add that involving parent volunteers also is a good idea. Keeping administrators, PTA members, and local news media informed of the project's existence and students' accomplishments is well worth the effort. Such informal public relations work can foster future project support and provision of additional Internet access at schools.

Step 8: Create Closure

All of the authors mentioned in this chapter suggest that telecomputing projects should end with a final, tangible product such as a Web page, written report, public presentation, videotape, or display. This product should be scheduled, completed, and shared with all participants, then made available to a larger, interested community.

The importance of this suggestion cannot be overstated. After all of the planning, coordination, collaboration, and hard work—and after all of the rich learning that took place—participants and others outside the project group should have the opportunity to marvel at what has been accomplished. Also, if plans for and results of the project can be made available through a Web page online, other teachers can learn from the project's design and implementation.

After the project is over, if time is available, students and teachers often enjoy informally sharing perspectives about and memories of different stages of the activity. It also is important to remember to allow time for everyone to say good-bye and thank you and perhaps to begin to consider working together in the future.

Creating "Virtual Spaces" for Projects

Telecollaborative projects happen both across and within participating school sites; they have no single geographic location. It is helpful, therefore, to create a central, virtual space for sharing information about project-related activities. Many project directors use World Wide Web pages for this purpose. At this point in the discussion of logistical and operational dimensions of telecomputing activities, planners should consider the design of these project pages, specifically considering the project-related purposes that they can serve.

Eliel Saarinen (1873-1950), a Finnish architect and city planner who moved to the United States in the 1920s, was quoted as saying, "Always design a thing by considering it in its next larger context—a chair in a room, a room in a house, a house in an environment, an environment in a city plan" (Tripp 1970, p. 149). Saarinen's words can apply to World Wide Web pages that support telecomputing projects. The "next larger context" for such pages is the variety of functions that designers intend the WWW site to serve and support. Pages should be created with these functions in mind, and project directors should answer questions like these before beginning work on the pages:

• Who will be interested in exploring the site?

• What types of information should be available at the site to address different audience interests?

• How should this information be presented so that it is most helpful to project participants or Web strollers?

Currently, Web page design is addressed primarily in terms of form and content, rather than function. We consider, for example, layout options (i.e., Should we use frames?); overall structure (i.e., One long page with links to subsections or multiple, shorter pages?); transfer time (i.e., How many graphics should I put on this page?); browser differences (i.e., Will Lynx users be able to benefit from my site?); readability (i.e., Does this combination of background pattern and text color make the page difficult to read?); and aesthetics (i.e., Is the combination of colors, items, and spacing pleasing to the eye?). However, planners also should consider project-related functions in designing WWW documents. After all, any architect (including Saarinen) would strongly suggest that form follows function.

Project-Related Page Functions

After reviewing several hundred K-12 project pages, I have identified 10 different project page functions. More information about projects cited that are still functioning is available on the Web using the URLs that follow:

Project Overview. Web sites can serve as succinct introductions to the goals and structures for telecomputing projects. For example, the Canadian Kids from Kanata project was overviewed on its Web page, offering a general description of this global classroom effort to encourage communication among indigenous peoples and later immigrants. The page included a brief history of the project, an explanation of how the groups are organized, summaries of praise that the project received in the past, supporting organizations and individuals, and links enabling visitors to fill out an application to participate or e-mail organizers with questions.

Project Announcement. Web sites can announce projects, inviting participation and providing links to relevant resources. The Chatback project collection, based in the United Kingdom, sponsored Memories from 1945. This activity helped senior citizens communicate with students about their memories of experiences during World War II. The main page for this project included fascinating introductions to the seniors available for communication (fig. 5.3). The page also included information on how to subscribe to the project's e-mail discussion list, links to stories about people's WWII experiences, and sample project work from students in Cottage Grove, Minnesota.

Project Instructions. Web sites can provide specific instructions on how to participate in a project. I*EARN has a well-organized page for its Learning Circle global classroom projects (http://www.iearn.org/iearn/circles/). It is supported by a hypertext-linked set of carefully

crafted and information-rich Web pages, which provide step-by-step instructions for project participation. A small section of the main page at this site appears in Figure 5.4. Please note the many links to documents supporting each stage of project work. The page also contains information on joining I*EARN, links to conferencing spaces in which project partners communicate, and a chronologically organized timeline for the current session of Learning Circletelecollaboration.

Information Repository and Exchange. Web sites can serve as places for project participants to exchange information. KIDLINK's

Figure 5.3
FROM MAIN PAGE OF THE CHATBACK PROJECT

"Those who do not learn from the past are condemned to repeat it"; George Santayana.

Many of the young people who lived in the year 1945 and the last years of World War Two are still alive. Time has healed the wounds on both sides, but some of those survivors want to be sure that the lessons of the past will be learned by a new generation.

The following people who lived in that time 50 years ago are available to share the experiences of their everyday life in the year 1945. Collectively, we are a living history book.

THE BERLIN SCHOOLBOY - who lived through the 1,000 bomber raids.
THE LONDON SCHOOLBOY - during the blitz and the doodle-bugs.
THE VIENNA SCHOOLGIRL - coping with discrimination under the Nazi regime.
THE WARSAW SCHOOLBOY - his father shot, his mother sent to Auschwitz.
THE SURVIVOR - living through the hell of Auschwitz.
THE POLISH EXILE - deported as a slave-labourer at age 14.
THE LAND GIRL - from university to hard labour as a Land Girl on a farm.
THE AMERICAN SOLDIER - in England, waiting to go to war.
THE RAF ENGINEER - keeping the fighters in fighting trim.
THE LOST CHILD FROM SIBERIA - with no memories of Mother or Father.
THE NURSE - escorting children from the dangers of 'the blitz'.
THE CANADIAN AIR FORCE OFFICER - helping a war-torn Europe to recover.
THE VIENNA SCHOOLBOY - growing up with the Russian occupation.
THE CROATIAN SOLDIER - forced to fight for the Nazis, who survived the 'Croatian Death March'.

They will **NOT** be waving flags, or glorifying war. They **WILL** be paying testimony to those who quietly endured and sometimes lost on **BOTH** sides of the conflict...

60

long-term Multi-Cultural Calendar database creation project site (http://www.kidlink.org/KIDPROJ/MCC/) cross-indexes student-written depictions of hundreds of holidays and festivals from around the world. The holiday descriptions are accessible by month, holiday name, country, and author. A World Wide Web form also is available at the site so that new entries for the holiday database can be submitted easily. A portion of this form is included in Figure 5.5.

Context for Project-Related Communication. Web pages can be constructed by project par-

ticipants, creating an open-ended form of multimedia communication. The Electronic Emissary telementoring project (http://www.tapr.org/emissary/), which matches volunteer subject-matter experts with students and teachers, has seen a few electronic teams create Web pages to facilitate their virtual interactions. This is especially effective when pictures or diagrams need to be viewed concurrently, and they can be supplemented by realtime audio or video interaction using CU-SeeMe.

For example, a meteorologist working for the National Center for Atmospheric Research

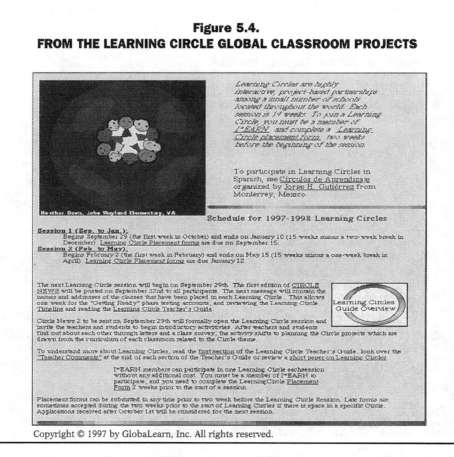

Figure 5.4.
FROM THE LEARNING CIRCLE GLOBAL CLASSROOM PROJECTS

in Colorado helped a 6th grade class in Texas learn about atmospheric science by suggesting an experiment that required the assembly of a device to help them "measure radiative processes." The scientist posted a picture of the device on the common page as a beginning to an ongoing, multimedia discussion of the results that the planned experiment yielded.

Project Support. Web sites can serve as organized collections of project-related resources. CoVis's rich and well-organized site (http://www.covis.nwu.edu/) offers a plethora

---

Figure 5.5.
FROM THE MULTI-CULTURAL CALENDAR DATABASE CREATION PROJECT

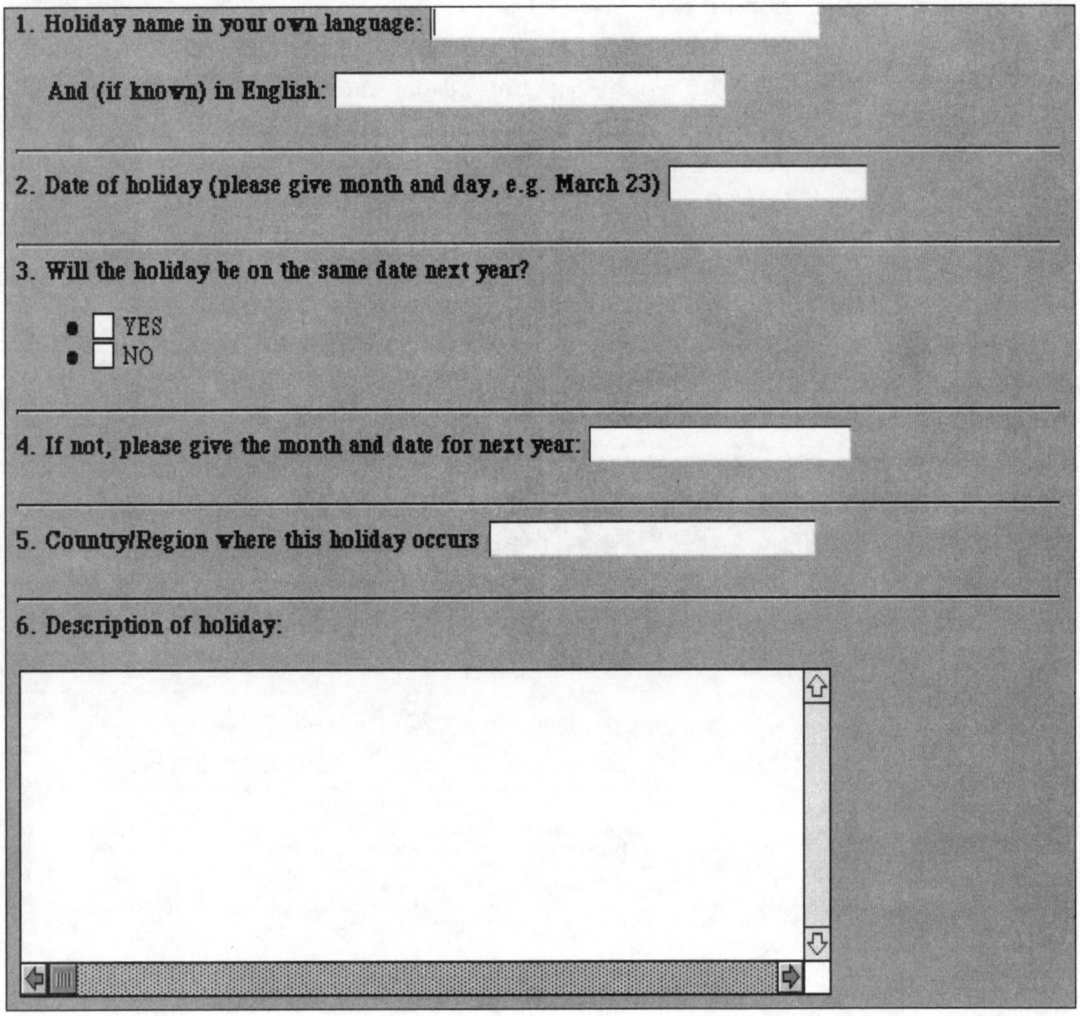

1. Holiday name in your own language: [   ]

   And (if known) in English: [   ]

2. Date of holiday (please give month and day, e.g. March 23) [   ]

3. Will the holiday be on the same date next year?

   ● ☐ YES
   ● ☐ NO

4. If not, please give the month and date for next year: [   ]

5. Country/Region where this holiday occurs [   ]

6. Description of holiday:

[   ]

of materials that participants can use as they explore geosciences in telementoring contexts, "learning through collaborative visualization." The key to making project support sites as useful as possible is to organize the materials for quick and efficient access. CoVis's main menu, shown in Figure 5.6, reflects the care and thought that project coordinators have put into designing the project's Web site.

Project Chronology. Web sites can present chronologies of past and ongoing project work. Figure 5.7 shows the beautiful page that greeted GlobaLearn's (http://www.globalearn. org/) Web site visitors in 1996.

Selecting the "Black Sea Expedition" icon (shown on p. 63) allowed viewers to see rich artifacts of many types that traced the experi-

ences of a group of students who traveled for eight weeks around the Black Sea, beginning and ending in Istanbul. In taking this trip and telecommunicating with students as they did so, the "expedition team" provided telefieldtrip opportunities for 5,000 other students from all over the world.

Showcase of Participants' Works. Web sites can provide viewing space to share project participants' creations. MidLink Magazine (http://longwood.cs.ucf.edu/~MidLink/), an electronic publishing project for middle grade students, publishes their art and writing four times each year. Each issue of this "e-zine" is actually a thematically linked collection of students' works that were associated with different telecomputing projects. Examples from

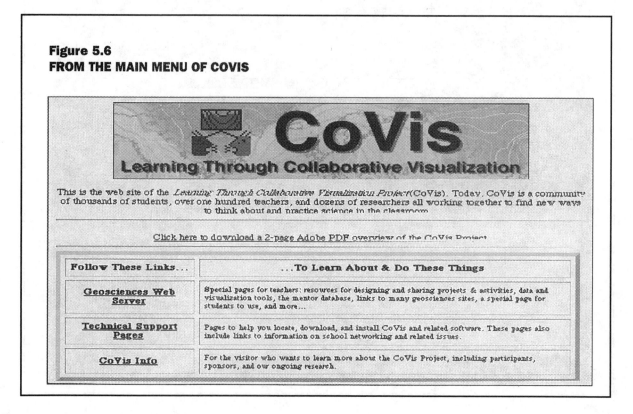

Figure 5.6
FROM THE MAIN MENU OF COVIS

Figure 5.7.
FROM THE GLOBALEARN PROJECT

one issue included stories, peace cards, a haiku exchange, and a virtual quilt, all relating to the theme of friendship.

Project Center. Web sites can also serve as multipurpose centers, combining several of the project-related functions listed earlier. The main menu for the Global SchoolNet's KidsPeak telefieldtrip project (http://www.gsn.org/past/kidspeak/index.html), which followed mountain climber Sandy Hill Pittman as she and her team ascended Mount Everest in 1996, illustrates how many of the page functions mentioned in this section can be combined to create an information-rich, easy to use, multipurpose "virtual center" for an educational telecomputing project (fig. 5.8).

Project-Spawning Service. Web sites can offer electronic services that help initiate new telecomputing projects. A growing number of services that help teachers and students locate information and interpersonal contacts for new projects are now available on the Web. Notable among these are locators for keypals and global classroom partners, such as:

• Classroom Connect's Teacher Contact Database (http://www.classroom.net/contact/);

• Email Classroom Exchange (http://www.iglou.com/xchange/ece/index.html);

• The Intercultural E-Mail Classroom Connections service (http://www.stolaf.edu/network/iecc/);

• Virtual Handshake (http://ananke.advanced.org/3174/), which offers interpersonal connections in seven different languages:

64

English, Spanish, French, German, Afrikaans, and both SJIS and rōma Japanese.

Hopefully, the pages described here will help teachers to allow function to drive form as they design Web sites to support current and future educational telecomputing projects. I would be remiss, however, if I did not urge us all to continue to follow Saarinen's sage advice by considering function in terms of its next larger context: purpose. For, as Norbert Wiener wrote in *The Human Use of Human Beings* (1954), "There is one quality more important than 'know-how' . . . . This is 'know-what,' by which we determine not only how to accomplish our purposes, but what our purposes are to be" (Tripp 1970, p. 524).

In the context of educational activity design, the "next larger purpose" always refers back to curriculum-based content and process goals. Telecomputing is not, and should not be treated as, another curriculum. Instead, it can serve teaching and learning goals in rich, authentic, and forward-thinking ways.

Granted, this chapter is filled with the nuts and bolts that must accompany activity designs if creative visions are to become educationally beneficial realities. Yet these many fine points are like the slender threads of a spider's web. An Ethiopian proverb illustrates the potential power of these threads: When spider webs unite, they can tie up a lion. Here's hoping that these suggestions, along with the others offered in this book, will help you to help your teachers start spinning some virtual, educational webs.

Figure 5.8.
FROM THE GLOBAL SCHOOLNET KIDSPEAK TELEFIELDTRIP PROJECT

Glossary

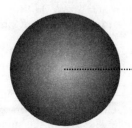

accountholder:
A person who has access to Internet services through a unique user name located on an Internet server somewhere in the world.

asynchronous:
Not simultaneous in time, such as the communication that occurs when folks send and receive e-mail messages or post items to public discussion groups on the Internet.

browser:
A piece of software that makes it possible for users to access information and services on the Internet, specifically using the organizational structure called the "World Wide Web." See "World Wide Web."

chats:
Realtime (synchronous) communication that occurs online. Can be text-based or audio/video.

connectivity:
Having the hardware, software, and wiring in place to support the use of Internet tools and resources.

CU-SeeMe:
A free piece of software, written by folks at Cornell University, that allows Internet users with high-speed online service (56 kilobits per second or higher) to see and hear one another. Requires use of a digital camera, such as the Connectix QuickCam.

cyberspace:
The collection of interconnected virtual "places" that are created when Internet resources and services are made available and are used by people.

66

electronic mail:
An Internet-based tool that allows accountholders to communicate with one another by sending and receiving private and/or public messages.

Global Matrix:
The largest collection of interconnected networks in the world that allow computer users to share information with one another in different forms. The Internet is part of the Global Matrix.

Gopher:
The World Wide Web's predecessor. Gophers are hierarchically organized menus of information that run on larger servers, allowing users to locate specific information without having to know its exact location.

Gopherspace:
The interconnected collection of Gophers, which reference one another, so that users can find information on the Internet without having to know specific Internet addresses/locations.

host:
A larger capacity computer connected to the Internet that is specially configured so that it can offer information (in the forms of World Wide Web pages, files, etc.) and (in many cases) personal accounts to Internet users.

hypertext:
Multimedia materials, including text, that are linked to one another in a nonlinear way, so that users can "jump" from one piece of information to another without having to follow a predetermined sequence.

information network:
A collection of computer hardware, interconnected by use of wires and/or other types of wireless connections, and distributed over a large geographic area, that, through use of software, makes information of many different types available to users.

Internaut:
Yvonne Andres' creative term for people who actively explore cyberspace, much like an astronaut explores new territories in outer space.

Internet:
The worldwide collection of interconnected information networks that allow computer users to share information with one another in different forms. The Internet is part of the Global Matrix. It is possible to have a user account on the Matrix without having full access to the Internet's resources. In these cases, users would be able to use, for example, electronic mail and World Wide Web browsers, but not be able to directly download files.

Internet Relay Chat (IRC):
A program supported on several large Internet servers that allows users from all over the world to "talk" with one another, by typing. When people use IRC, they select "channels" on which to communicate. People who are on the same channel at the same time can chat by typing.

links:
Those elements on World Wide Web pages that allow users to "travel" electronically to other places on the Internet that are related to what is currently being displayed on the page. See "hypertext."

listserv:
Technically, this is a piece of software that runs on a larger capacity computer connected to the Internet that allows single messages to be copied and distributed to many different e-mail addresses. Although there are other such programs (such as majordomo), "listserv" has come to be used as the generic word.

newsgroups:
Virtual, public places in cyberspace in which users can engage in asynchronous public discussions. Newsgroups can be available Internet-wide, but most that teachers and students use are set up for local or regional clientele.

online:
The state of currently using Internet tools or resources of any type.

realtime:
Simultaneous in time, such as the kind of communication that use of IRC or CU-SeeMe allows. "Realtime" and "synchronous" are synonyms, but "realtime" is a more commonly used term.

search engine:
A program available on the World Wide Web that allows users to locate specific information without having to browse to find it, or know the World Wide

Web page address on which the information is located.

server:
See "host." More often, servers offer personal account services to users. "Host" is a more general term, in some communications circles.

synchronous:
Occurring simultaneously in time. See "realtime."

tele-:
A prefix meaning "at a distance." Therefore, "telecommunications" means "communications done at a distance."

telecollaboration:
Using a computer connected to a telecommunications network, like the Internet, to collaborate with others at a distance.

telecomputing:
Using a computer to do telecommunications.

teleresearch:
Using a computer connected to a telecommunications network, like the Internet, to do research at a distance.

URL:
Uniform Resource Locator; a unique address for a collection of information on the Internet. URLs are often referred to as "Web addresses," differentiated from electronic mail addresses. URLs can refer to WWW pages, Gophers, file archives, newsgroups, and interactively accessible resources, such as online databases.

video conferences:
Realtime communications among two or more locations that occur online using video and audio, rather than text. See "CU-SeeMe."

World Wide Web:
An easy-to-use way of organizing access to and displaying information in many forms (e.g., text, still pictures, video clips, audio files) on the Internet. Abbreviated as "Web" or "WWW." See "browser."

Online Resources for Educational Telecomputing Projects

Indexes to Online Projects and Activities

Access Excellence Activities Exchange
http://www.gene.com/ae/AE/

Adventure Online
http://www.adventureonline.com/

The BIG PAGE of School Internet Projects
http://www.mts.net/~jgreenco/internet.html#
Classroom

Blue Web'n Applications Library
http://www.kn.pacbell.com/wired/bluewebn/

British Council InterLink
http://www.interlink.org.nz/

Busy Teachers' K-12 Web Site
http://www.ceismc.gatech.edu/BusyT/TOC.html

Electronic Elementary Magazine
http://www.inform.umd.edu/EdRes/Topic/
Education/K-12/MDK12_Stuff/homepers/emag/

ENO/REO Student Projects
http://www.enoreo.on.ca/mars97/index.htm

EnviroNet (environmental monitoring pooled data
activities)
http://earth.simmons.edu/

Global SchoolNet's Internet Projects Registry
http://www.gsn.org/pr/index.html

The GrassRoots Program
http://www.schoolnet.ca/grassroots/

Houghton-Mifflin's Online Projects Center
http://www.hmco.com/hmco/school/projects/
index.html

I*EARN
http://www.iearn.org/iearn/

KIDPROJ
http://www.kidlink.org/KIDPROJ/

Learning Circles (IEARN)
http://www.ed.uiuc.edu/guidelines/Riel-93.html

Los Angeles County TEAMS Projects
http://teams.lacoe.edu/documentation/
projects/projects.html

Math Forum
http://forum.swarthmore.edu/

NASA K-12 Internet Initiative: Online Interactive
Projects
http://quest.arc.nasa.gov/interactive/

National Student Research Center
http://yn.la.ca.us/nsrc/nsrc.html

New Zealand Education Web
http://www.cwa.co.nz/index.html

NickNacks: Telecollaborations
http://www1.minn.net:80/~schubert/
EdHelpers.html

Oceanography Projects
http://seawifs.gsfc.nasa.gov/

oz-TeacherNet Web Site
http://owl.qut.edu.au/oz-teachernet/index.html

Passport to Knowledge (electronic fieldtrips)
http://quest.arc.nasa.gov/antarctica/passport.html

RouteICS Projects
http://ics.soe.umich.edu/

Telemation Project
http://www.telis.org/telis/telemat/telemat.htm

United Nations CyberSchoolBus
http://www.un.org/Pubs/CyberSchoolBus/
main.htm

Virginia's PEN Resources
http://pen.k12.va.us/

David Warlick's Projects ("Global Grocery List,"
etc.)
http://www.landmark-project.com/eco-market.
html

The Wild Ones (wildlife projects)
http://www.columbia.edu/cu/cerc/WildOnes/

Writers In Electronic Residence (WIER)
http://www.edu.yorku.ca/wierhome/

Guides to Online Activity Development

AT&T Learning Circles Teacher Guide
http://www.att.com/education/lcguide/

"Conceptual Frameworks for Network Learning
Environments" (article)
http://www.ed.uiuc.edu/TTa/Papers/JL_EdTele/

CyberConnections
http://www.esc13.tenet.edu/cc/cc.html

GlobalQuest II: Teaching With The Internet
http://quest.arc.nasa.gov/globalquest2/index.html

Houghton-Mifflin Activity Design Tips
http://www.hmco.com/hmco/school/projects/
how2.html

"Keys to Successful Projects" (article)
http://www.ed.uiuc.edu/guidelines/Rogers.html

NickNacks: Collaborative Project Planner
http://www1.minn.net:80/~schubert/
NNplanner.html

"Observations on Educational Electronic
Networks" (article)
http://lrs.ed.uiuc.edu/guidelines/LRWS.html

"Organizing Educational Network Interactions:
Steps Towards a Theory of Network-Based

70

Learning Environments (article)"
http://www.ed.uiuc.edu/Guidelines/Levin-AERA-18Ap95.html

"Organizing Electronic Network-Based Instructional Interactions" (article)
http://www.ed.uiuc.edu/Guidelines/WLS.html

TENET Curriculum Infusion Guide
http://www.tenet.edu/tenet-info/ciguide/

Correspondent Locators

Classroom Connect's Teacher Contact Database
http://www.classroom.net/contact/

Electronic Emissary Project
http://www.tapr.org/emissary/

EMail Classroom Exchange
http://www.iglou.com/xchange/ece/index.html

HP Email Mentor Program
http://mentor.external.hp.com/

Intercultural E-Mail Classroom Connections
http://www.stolaf.edu/network/iecc/

Mighty Media KeyPals Club
http://www.mightymedia.com/keypals/

Virtual Handshake
http://ananke.advanced.org/3174/

Curriculum Content Resources Directories

Busy Teachers' K-12 Web Site
http://www.ceismc.gatech.edu/BusyT/TOC.html

Study WEB
http://www.studyweb.com

Teacher Resource Center
http://www.he.net/~tobrien/teacher.html

Teacher Topics
http://www.asd.k12.ak.us/Homepages/JAndrews/TeacherTopics.html

WebEd Curriculum Links
http://www.dpi.state.wi.us/dpi/dlcl/pld/WebEd.html

K-12 Telecomputing Publications

From Now On
http://fromnowon.org

National School Network Newsletter
http://nsn.bbn.com/news/newsletters/

NetTeach News Online
http://www.chaos.com/netteach/index.html

The Well Connected Educator
http://www.gsh.org/wce/

General K-12 Telecomputing Information

Acceptable Use Policies
http://www.erehwon.com/k12aup/

Classroom Connect
http://www.classroom.net/

ED's Oasis
http://www.EDsOasis.org/Oasis.html

Internet Compass for Schools
http://www.moms.com/index.html

Sally Laughon's Resource List
http://infoserver.etl.vt.edu/~/laughon/

Learning Resources Server
http://www.ed.uiuc.edu/

Learning With Technology Profile Tool
http://www.ncrtec.org/capacity/profile/profile.htm

Kathy Schrock's Guide for Educators
http://www.capecod.net/schrockguide/

Virtual Village Teachers' Lounge
    http://www.intergo.com/school/teacher.htm

"Way Cool" Education Sites
    http://www.webscout.com/

Web 66
    http://web66.coled.umn.edu/

71

References

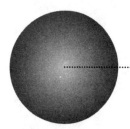

Briggs, L.J., ed. (1977). *Instructional Design: Principles and Applications*. Englewood Cliffs, N.J.: Educational Technology Publications.

Calcari, S. (1994). "A Snapshot of the Internet." *Internet World* 5, 6: 54–58.

Clark, R.E. (1983). "Reconsidering Research on Learning from Media." *Review of Educational Research* 53, 4: 445–459.

Doty, R. (1995). "Teacher's Aid." *Internet World* 6, 3: 75–77.

Fox, S. (1991). "The Production and Distribution of Knowledge Through Open and Distance Learning." In *Paradigms Regained: The Uses of Illuminative, Semiotic, and Post-Modern Criticism as Modes of Inquiry in Educational Technology*, edited by D. Hylnka and J.C. Belland, pp. 217-239. Englewood Cliffs, N.J.: Educational Technology Publications.

Gallo, M. (1994). "Assessing the Effect on High School Teachers of Direct and Unrestricted Access to the Internet: A Case Study of an East Central Florida High School." *Educational Technology Research and Development* 42, 4: 17–39.

Gunter, M.A., T.H. Estes, and J.H. Schwab. (1990). *Instruction: A Models Approach*. Boston: Allyn and Bacon.

Heaviside, S., T. Riggins, and E. Farris. (1997). *Advanced Telecommunications in U.S. Public Elementary and Secondary Schools, Fall 1996* (E.D. TABS Publication No. NCES 97-944). Washington, D.C.: U.S. Government Printing Office.

Joyce, B., and M. Weil. (1972). *Models of Teaching*. Englewood Cliffs, N.J.: Prentice-Hall.

Joyce, B., and M. Weil. (1986). *Models of Teaching*. 3rd ed. Englewood Cliffs, N.J.: Prentice-Hall.

Jupiter Communications, Inc. (1997). *The 1997 Online Kids Report* [Online]. Available: http://www.jup.com/tracks/content/

Lincoln, W., and M. Suid. (1986). *The Teacher's Quotation Book*. Palo Alto, Calif.: Dale Seymour Publications.

McKinney, E. (1995). "How Many People Join the Internet Each Day?" *Matrix News* 5, 10: 1.

"Millions Hooked on the Net." (April 1995). *NetGuide* 2, 4: 139.

National Institute of Standards and Technology. (1994). *Putting the Information Infrastructure to Work: Report of the Information Infrastructure Task Force Committee on Applications and Technology*. Washington, D.C.: U.S. Department of Commerce.

Quarterman, J.S. (1997a). "Country Counts for January 1997." *Matrix News* 7, 4: 9.

Quarterman, J.S. (1997b). "1997 Users and Hosts of the Internet and the Matrix." *Matrix News* 7, 1: 4.

Riel, M. (1992). "Telecommunications: Avoiding the Black Hole." *The Computing Teacher* 19, 4: 16–17.

Riel, M.M., and J.A. Levin. (1990). "Building Electronic Communities: Success and Failure in Computer Networking." *Instructional Science* 19: 145–169.

Rogers, A., Y. Andres, M. Jacks, and T. Clausen. (1990). "Keys to Successful Telecomputing." *The Computing Teacher* 17, 8: 25–28.

Rogers, E.M. (1986). *Communication Technology: The New Media in Society*. New York: The Free Press.

Rogers, E.M. (1995). *Diffusion of Innovations*. 4th ed. New York: The Free Press.

Strain, J.E. (1986). "Method: Design-Procedure Versus Method-Technique." *System* 14, 3: 287–294.

Taylor, W.D., and J.D. Swartz. (1991). "Whose Knowledge?" In *Paradigms Regained: The Uses of Illuminative, Semiotic, and Post-Modern Criticism as Modes of Inquiry in Educational Technology*, edited by D. Hylnka and J.C. Belland, pp. 51-62. Englewood Cliffs, N.J.: Educational Technology Publications.

Tripp, R.T. (1970). *The International Thesaurus of Quotations*. New York: Thomas Y. Crowell, Publishers.

Waugh, M.L., J.A. Levin, and K. Smith. (1994). "Network-Based Instructional Interactions, Part 2: Interpersonal Strategies." *The Computing Teacher* 21, 6: 48–50.

73

Index

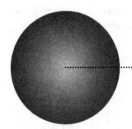

Page numbers with an *"f"* after them refer to pages that contain figures.

77

About the Author

Judi Harris is a faculty member in Curriculum and Instruction at the University of Texas at Austin, teaching graduate-level courses in both instructional technology and nonpositivistic research methods. Judi directs "The Electronic Emissary" (http://www.tapr.org/emissary/), a K-12 curriculum-oriented telementoring service and research effort. She also leads professional development programs and speaks to educators in the U.S. and Canada about telecomputing. Judi has authored *Way of the Ferret: Finding and Using Educational Resources on the Internet* (ISTE), *Teaching and Learning with the Internet* (ASCD), and more than 130 articles on curriculum-based applications of educational technologies. Her new book for classroom teachers, *Virtual Architecture: Designing and Directing Curriculum-Based Telecomputing* (ISTE), was released in late 1997.

Originally (and forever) an elementary-level classroom teacher and K-6 mathematics/computer specialist, Judi earned her Ph.D. in Instructional Technology from the University of Virginia.

She may be contacted at the Department of Curriculum and Instruction, 406 Sanchez Building, University of Texas at Austin, Austin, TX 78712-1294.